The Student's Essential Formula Book

Mathematical Formulas, Tables, Puzzles and Curios

1st Edition

Compilation by

John C. Sparks

authorHOUSE

1663 LIBERTY DRIVE, SUITE 200
BLOOMINGTON, INDIANA 47403
(800) 839-8640
www.authorhouse.com

First published by AuthorHouse 06/23/04

ISBN: 1-4184-5786-8 (e)
ISBN: 1-4184-5785-X (sc)

Library of Congress Control Number: 2004094184

Printed in the United States of America
Bloomington, Indiana

This book is printed on acid-free paper.

Forward

Formulas, they seem to be the bane of every beginning mathematics student who has yet to realize that formulas are about structure and relationship—and not about memorization. Granted, formulas have to be memorized; for, it is partly through memorization that we eventually become 'unconsciously competent'. This means we are a true master of our skill, practicing it in an almost effortless, automatic sense. In mathematics, this means we have mastered the underlying algebraic language to the same degree that we have mastered our native tongue. Knowing formulas and understanding the reasoning behind them propels one towards the road to mathematical mastery, so essential in our modern high-tech society.

This book consists of three major sections. Section I—Formulas—contains most of the formulas that you would expect to encounter through the first year of college (and perhaps the second) regardless of major. In addition, there are formulas rarely seen in such compilations, included as a mathematical treat for the inquisitive. Section II—Tables—includes both 'pure math' tables and physical-science tables, useful in a variety of disciples ranging from physics to nursing. As in Section I, some tables are included just to nurture curiosity in a spirit of fun. *Fun in discovery definitely should be a part of our learning experience in mathematics.* Section III—Puzzles and Curios—is all fun! Here, I have pulled together a variety of mathematical wonders and puzzles collected over three decades of teaching.

I would like to thank Mr. Al Giambrone—Chairman of the Department of Mathematics, Sinclair Community College, Dayton, Ohio—for providing required-memorization formula lists for 22 Sinclair mathematics courses from which the formula compilation was partially built. In addition, I would like to thank Mr. Vince Miller—Adjunct Professor, Department of Mathematics, Sinclair Community College—for providing a careful and exacting review of the final manuscript.

John C. Sparks
December 2004

3

Dedication

I would like to dedicate this work
to my wife and family—
Carolyn, Robert, and Curtis Sparks.
Also... to the Ultimate Mathematician.

Significance

The wisp in my glass on a clear winter's night
Is home for a billion wee glimmers of light,
Each crystal itself one faraway dream
With faraway worlds surrounding its gleam.

And locked in the realm of each tiny sphere
Is all that is met through an eye or an ear;
Too, all that is felt by a hand or our love,
For we are but whits in the sea seen above.

Such scales immense make wonder abound
And make a lone knee touch the cold ground.
For what is this man that he should be made
To sing to The One whose breath heavens laid?

July 1999

5

Table of Contents

Part I: Formulas

Part II: Tables

2) Physical Sciences — 71

Part III: Puzzles and Curios

1) Puzzles — 82

Part I

Formulas

1) Algebra

1.1 Field Axioms

The field axioms *decree* the fundamental operating properties of the real number system and provide the basis for all advanced operating properties in mathematics.

Let a, b & c be any three real numbers		
Properties	**Addition**	**Multiplication**
Closure	$a + b$ is a unique real number	$a \cdot b$ is a unique real number
Commutative	$a + b = b + a$	$a \cdot b = b \cdot a$
Associative	$(a + b) + c =$ $a + (b + c)$	$(ab)c =$ $a(bc)$
Identity	$0 \Rightarrow a + 0 = a$	$1 \Rightarrow a \cdot 1 = a$
Inverse	$a \Rightarrow a + (-a) = 0$ $\Rightarrow (-a) + a = 0$	$a \neq 0 \Rightarrow a \cdot \frac{1}{a} = 1$ $\Rightarrow \frac{1}{a} \cdot a = 1$
Distributive *or* *Linking Property*	$a \cdot (b + c) = a \cdot b + a \cdot c$	
Note: $ab = a(b) = (a)b$ are alternate representations of $a \cdot b$		

1.2 Divisibility Tests

DIVISOR	CONDITION THAT MAKES IT SO
2	The last digit is 0,2,4,6, or 8
3	The sum of the digits is divisible by 3
4	The last two digits are divisible by 4
5	The last digit is 0 or 5
6	The number is divisible by both 2 and 3
7	The number formed by adding five times the last digit to the remaining digits is divisible by 7**
8	The last three digits are divisible by 8
9	The sum of the digits is divisible by 9
10	The last digit is 0
11	11 divides the number formed by subtracting two times the last digit from the remaining digits**
12	The number is divisible by both 3 and 4
13	13 divides the number formed by adding four times the last digit to the remaining digits**
14	The number is divisible by both 2 and 7
15	The number is divisible by both 3 and 5
17	17 divides the number formed by subtracting five times the last digit from the remaining digits**
19	19 divides the number formed by adding two times the last digit to the remaining digits**
23	23 divides the number formed by adding seven times the last digit to the remaining digits**
29	29 divides the number formed by adding three times the last digit to the remaining digits**
31	31 divides the number formed by subtracting three times the last digit from the remaining digits**
37	37 divides the number formed by subtracting eleven times the last digit from the remaining digits**
**These tests are iterative tests in that you continue to cycle through the process until a number is formed that can be easily divided by the divisor in question.	

1.3 Subtraction and Division

1. Definitions

Subtraction: $a - b \equiv a + (-b)$

Division: $a \div b \equiv a \cdot \dfrac{1}{b}$

2. Alternate representation of $a \div b$: $a \div b = \dfrac{a}{b}$

3. Division Properties of Zero

Zero in numerator: $a \neq 0 \Rightarrow \dfrac{0}{a} = 0$

Zero in denominator: $\dfrac{a}{0}$ is undefined!

Zero in both: $\dfrac{0}{0}$ is undefined!

1.4 Rules for Fractions

Let $\dfrac{a}{b}$ and $\dfrac{c}{d}$ be fractions with $b \neq 0$ and $d \neq 0$.

1. Equality: $\dfrac{a}{b} = \dfrac{c}{d} \Leftrightarrow ad = bc$

2. Equivalency: $c \neq 0 \Rightarrow \dfrac{a}{b} = \dfrac{ac}{bc} = \dfrac{ca}{cb} = \dfrac{ac}{cb} = \dfrac{ca}{bc}$

3. Addition (like denominators): $\dfrac{a}{b} + \dfrac{c}{b} = \dfrac{a+c}{b}$

4. Addition (unlike denominators):

$$\dfrac{a}{b} + \dfrac{c}{d} = \dfrac{ad}{bd} + \dfrac{cb}{bd} = \dfrac{ad + cb}{bd}$$

14

5. Subtraction (like denominators): $\dfrac{a}{b} - \dfrac{c}{b} = \dfrac{a-c}{b}$

6. Subtraction (unlike denominators):

$$\dfrac{a}{b} - \dfrac{c}{d} = \dfrac{ad}{bd} - \dfrac{cb}{bd} = \dfrac{ad - cb}{bd}$$

7. Multiplication: $\dfrac{a}{b} \cdot \dfrac{c}{d} = \dfrac{ac}{bd}$

8. Division: $c \neq 0 \Rightarrow \dfrac{a}{b} \div \dfrac{c}{d} = \dfrac{a}{b} \cdot \dfrac{d}{c} = \dfrac{ad}{bc}$

9. Reduction of Complex Fraction: $\dfrac{\frac{a}{b}}{\frac{c}{d}} = \dfrac{a}{b} \div \dfrac{c}{d}$

10. Placement of Sign: $-\dfrac{a}{b} = \dfrac{-a}{b} = \dfrac{a}{-b}$

1.5 Rules for Exponents

1. Addition: $a^n a^m = a^{n+m}$

2. Subtraction: $\dfrac{a^n}{a^m} = a^{n-m}$

3. Multiplication: $(a^n)^m = a^{nm}$

4. Distributed over a Simple Product: $(ab)^n = a^n b^n$

5. Distributed over a Complex Product: $(a^m b^p)^n = a^{mn} b^{pn}$

6. Distributed over a Simple Quotient: $\left(\dfrac{a}{b}\right)^n = \dfrac{a^n}{b^n}$

7. Distributed over a Complex Quotient: $\left(\dfrac{a^m}{b^p}\right)^n = \dfrac{a^{mn}}{b^{pn}}$

8. Definition of Negative Exponent: $\dfrac{1}{a^n} \equiv a^{-n}$

9. Definition of Radical Expression: $\sqrt[n]{a} \equiv a^{\frac{1}{n}}$

10. Definition when No Exponent is Present: $a = a^1$

11. Definition of Zero Exponent: $a^0 = 1$

1.6 Factor Formulas

1. Simple Common Factor: $ab + ac = a(b+c) = (b+c)a$
2. Grouped Common Factor:
$$ab + ac + db + dc = (b+c)a + d(b+c) =$$
$$(b+c)a + (b+c)d = (b+c)(a+d)$$
3. Difference of Squares: $a^2 - b^2 = (a+b)(a-b)$
4. Sum of Squares: $a^2 + b^2 = (a+bi)(a-bi)$
5. Perfect Square: $a^2 \pm 2ab + b^2 = (a \pm b)^2$
6. General Trinomial: $x^2 + (a+b)x + ab = (x+a)(x+b)$
7. Sum of Cubes: $a^3 + b^3 = (a+b)(a^2 - ab + b^2)$
8. Difference of Cubes: $a^3 - b^3 = (a-b)(a^2 + ab + b^2)$
9. Power Reduction to an Integer:
$$a^4 + a^2b^2 + b^4 = (a^2 + ab + b^2)(a^2 - ab + b^2)$$
10. Power Reduction to a Radical: $x^2 - a = (x - \sqrt{a})(x + \sqrt{a})$
11. Power Reduction to an Integer plus a Radical:
$$a^2 + ab + b^2 = (a + \sqrt{ab} + b)(a - \sqrt{ab} + b)$$

1.7 Laws of Equality

Let $A = B$ be an algebraic equality and C, D be any quantities.

1. Addition: $A + C = B + C$

2. Subtraction: $A - C = B - C$

3. Multiplication: $A \cdot C = B \cdot C$

4. Division: $\dfrac{A}{C} = \dfrac{B}{C}$ provided $C \neq 0$

5. Exponent: $A^n = B^n$ provided n is an integer

6. Reciprocal: $\dfrac{1}{A} = \dfrac{1}{B}$ provided $A \neq 0, B \neq 0$

7. Means & Extremes: $\dfrac{C}{A} = \dfrac{D}{B} \Rightarrow CB = AD$ if $A \neq 0, B \neq 0$

8. Zero Product Property: $A \cdot B = 0$ if and only if
$A = 0$ or $B = 0$

1.8 Rules for Radicals

1. Basic Definitions: $\sqrt[n]{a} \equiv a^{\frac{1}{n}}$ and $\sqrt[2]{a} \equiv \sqrt{a} \equiv a^{\frac{1}{2}}$

2. Complex Radical: $\sqrt[n]{a^m} = a^{\frac{m}{n}}$

3. Associative: $\left(\sqrt[n]{a}\right)^m = \sqrt[n]{a^m} = a^{\frac{m}{n}}$

4. Simple Product: $\sqrt[n]{a}\sqrt[n]{b} = \sqrt[n]{ab}$

5. Simple Quotient: $\dfrac{\sqrt[n]{a}}{\sqrt[n]{b}} = \sqrt[n]{\dfrac{a}{b}}$

6. Complex Product: $\sqrt[n]{a}\sqrt[m]{b} = \sqrt[nm]{a^m b^n}$

7. Complex Quotient: $\dfrac{\sqrt[n]{a}}{\sqrt[m]{b}} = \sqrt[nm]{\dfrac{a^m}{b^n}}$

8. Nesting: $\sqrt[n]{\sqrt[m]{a}} = \sqrt[nm]{a}$

9. Rationalization Rules for $n > m$

Numerator: $\dfrac{\sqrt[n]{a^m}}{b} = \dfrac{a}{b\sqrt[n]{a^{n-m}}}$ Denominator: $\dfrac{b}{\sqrt[n]{a^m}} = \dfrac{b\sqrt[n]{a^{n-m}}}{a}$

1.9 Order of Operations

Step 1: Perform all power raisings in the order they occur from left to right

Step 2: Perform all multiplications and divisions in the order they occur from left to right

Step 3: Perform all additions and subtractions in the order they occur from left to right

Step 4: If parentheses are present, first perform steps 1 through 3 *on an as-needed basis* within the innermost set of parentheses until a single number is achieved. Then perform steps 1 through 3 (*again, on an as-needed basis*) for the next level of parentheses until all parentheses have been systematically removed.

Step 5: If a fraction bar is present, simultaneously perform steps 1 through 4 for the numerator and denominator, treating each as totally separate problem until a single number is achieved. Once single numbers have been achieved for both the numerator and the denominator, then a final division can be performed.

1.10 Three Meanings of 'Equals'

1. **Equals** is the mathematical equivalent of the English verb "is", the fundamental verb of being. A simple but subtle use of equals in this fashion is $2 = 2$.

2. **Equals** implies an equivalency of naming in that the same underlying quantity is being named in two different ways. This can be illustrated by the expression $2003 = MMIII$. Here, the two diverse symbols on both sides of the equals sign refer to the same and exact underlying quantity.

3. **Equals** states the product (either intermediate or final) that results from a process or action. For example, in the expression $2 + 2 = 4$, we are adding two numbers on the left-hand side of the equals sign. Here, addition can be viewed as a process or action between the numbers 2 and 2. The result or product from this process or action is the single number 4, which appears on the right-hand side of the equals sign.

18

1.11 Rules for Logarithms

1. Definition of Logarithm to Base $b > 0$: $y = \log_b x$
   if and only if $b^y = x$

2. Logarithm of the Same Base: $\log_b b = 1$

3. Logarithm of One: $\log_b 1 = 0$

4. Logarithm of the Base to a Power: $\log_b b^p = p$

5. Base to the Logarithm: $b^{\log_b p} = p$

6. Notation for Logarithm Base 10: $Log x = \log_{10} x$

7. Notation for Logarithm Base e: $\ln x = \log_e x$

8. Product: $\log_b(MN) = \log_b N + \log_b M$

9. Quotient: $\log_b\left(\dfrac{M}{N}\right) = \log_b M - \log_b N$

10. Power: $\log_b N^p = p \log_b N$

11: Change of Base Formula: $\log_b N = \dfrac{\log_a N}{\log_a b}$

1.12 Complex Numbers

1. Properties of the imaginary unit i: $i^2 = -1 \Rightarrow i = \sqrt{-1}$

2. Definition of Complex Number: Numbers of the form
   $a + bi$ where a, b are real numbers

4. Definition of Complex Conjugate: $\overline{a + bi} = a - bi$

5. Definition of Complex Modulus: $|a + bi| = \sqrt{a^2 + b^2}$

6. Addition: $(a + bi) + (c + di) = (a + c) + (b + d)i$

7. Subtraction: $(a + bi) - (c + di) = (a - c) + (b - d)i$

19

8. Multiplication:
$$(a+bi)(c+di) = ac+(ad+bc)i+bdi^2 =$$
$$ac-bd+(ad+bc)i$$

9: Division:
$$\frac{a+bi}{c+di} = \frac{(a+bi)\overline{(c+di)}}{(c+di)(c+di)} = \frac{(a+bi)(c-di)}{(c+di)(c-di)}$$
$$\frac{(ac+bd)+(bc-ad)i}{c^2-d^2} = \frac{ac+bd}{c^2-d^2}+\left(\frac{bc-ad}{c^2-d^2}\right)i$$

1.13 Quadratic Equations and Functions

Let $ax^2+bx+c = 0, a \neq 0$ be a quadratic equation

1. Quadratic Formula for Solutions x: $x = \dfrac{-b \pm \sqrt{b^2-4ac}}{2a}$

2. Solution Discriminator: b^2-4ac

    Two real solutions: $b^2-4ac > 0$
    One real solution: $b^2-4ac = 0$
    Two complex solutions: $b^2-4ac < 0$

3. Solution when $a = 0 \ \& \ b \neq 0$: $bx+c = 0 \Rightarrow x = \dfrac{-c}{b}$

4. Definition of Quadratic-in-Form Equation:
    $aw^2+bw+c = 0$ where w is a algebraic expression

5. Definition of Quadratic Function: $f(x) = ax^2+bx+c$

6. Axis of Symmetry for Quadratic Function: $x = \dfrac{-b}{2a}$

7. Vertex for Quadratic Function: $\left(\dfrac{-b}{2a}, \dfrac{4ac-b^2}{4a}\right)$

20

1.14 Cardano's Cubic Solution

Let $ax^3 + bx^2 + cx + d = 0$ be a cubic equation.

Step 1: Set $x = y - \dfrac{b}{3a}$

After this substitution, the above cubic becomes $y^3 + py + q = 0$
where

$$p = \left[\frac{c}{a} - \frac{b^2}{3a^2} \right] \And q = \left[\frac{2b^2}{27a^3} - \frac{bc}{3a^2} + \frac{d}{a} \right].$$

Step 2: Define u, v such that $y = u - v \And p = 3uv$

Step 3: Substitute for $y \And p$ in the equation $y^3 + py + q = 0$.
This leads to

$$(u^3)^2 + qu^3 - \frac{p^3}{27} = 0, \text{ which is quadratic-in-form in } u^3.$$

Step 4: Solve for $u^3 = \dfrac{-q + \sqrt{q^2 + \frac{4}{27}p^3}}{2}$

Step 5: Solve for $u \And v$ where $v = \dfrac{p}{3u}$ to obtain

$$u = \sqrt[3]{\frac{-q + \sqrt{q^2 + \frac{4}{27}p^3}}{2}}$$

$$v = -\sqrt[3]{\frac{-q - \sqrt{q^2 + \frac{4}{27}p^3}}{2}}$$

Step 6: Solve for x where $x = y - \dfrac{b}{3a} = u - v - \dfrac{b}{3a}$

21

1.15 Theory of Polynomial Equations

Let $P(x) = a_n x^n + a_{n-1} x^{n-1} + \ldots + a_2 x^2 + a_1 x + a_0$
be a polynomial written in standard form.

Eight Basic Theorems

1. Fundamental Theorem of Algebra: Every polynomial $P(x)$ of degree $N \geq 1$ has at least one solution x_0 for which $P(x_0) = 0$. This solution may be real or complex (i.e. has the form $a + bi$).

2. Numbers Theorem for Roots and Turning Points: If $P(x)$ is a polynomial of degree N, then the equation $P(x) = 0$ has up to N real solutions or *roots*. The equation $P(x) = 0$ has exactly N roots if one counts complex solutions of the form $a + bi$. Lastly, the graph of $P(x)$ will have up to $N - 1$ turning points (which includes both relative maxima and minima).

3. Real Root Theorem: If $P(x)$ is of odd degree having all real coefficients, then $P(x)$ has at least one real root.

4. Rational Root Theorem: If $P(x)$ has all integer coefficients, then any rational roots for the equation $P(x) = 0$ must have the form $\frac{p}{q}$ where p is a factor of the constant coefficient a_0 and q is a factor of the lead coefficient a_n. *Note: This result is used to form a rational-root possibility list.*

5. Complex Conjugate Pair Root Theorem: Suppose $P(x)$ has all real coefficients. If $a + bi$ is a root for $P(x)$ with $P(a + bi) = 0$, then $P(a - bi) = 0$.

6. Irrational Surd Pair Root Theorem: Suppose $P(x)$ has all rational coefficients. If $a + \sqrt{b}$ is a root for $P(x)$ with $P(a + \sqrt{b}) = 0$, then $P(a - \sqrt{b}) = 0$. *Note: the surd for the radical expression $a \pm \sqrt{b}$ is defined to be the quantity $a \mp \sqrt{b}$.*

7. Remainder Theorem: If $P(x)$ is divided by $(x-c)$, then the remainder R is equal to $P(c)$. *Note: this result is extensively used to evaluate a given polynomial $P(x)$ at various values of x.*

8. Factor Theorem: If c is any number with $P(c) = 0$, then $(x-c)$ is a factor of $P(x)$. This means $P(x) = (x-c) \cdot Q(x)$ where $Q(x)$ is a new, reduced polynomial having degree one less than $P(x)$. The converse is also true $P(x) = (x-c) \cdot Q(x) \Rightarrow P(c) = 0$.

Four Advanced Theorems

9. Root Location Theorem: Let (a,b) be an interval on the x axis with $P(a) \cdot P(b) < 0$. Then there is a value $x_0 \in (a,b)$ such that $P(x_0) = 0$.

10. Root Bounding Theorem: Divide $P(x)$ by $(x-d)$ to obtain $P(x) = (x-d) \cdot Q(x) + R$. Case $d > 0$: If both R and all the coefficients of $Q(x)$ are positive, then $P(x)$ has no root $x_0 > d$. Case $d < 0$: If the roots of $Q(x)$ alternate in sign—with the remainder R "in sync" at the end—then $P(x)$ has no root $x_0 < d$. *Note: Coefficients of zero can be counted either as positive or negative—which ever way helps in the subsequent determination.*

11. Descartes' Rule of Signs: Arrange $P(x)$ in standard order as shown in the title bar. The number of positive real solutions equals the number of coefficient sign variations or that number decreased by an even number. Likewise, the number of negative real solutions equals the number of coefficient sign variations in $P(-x)$ or that number decreased by an even number.

12. Turning Point Theorem: Let a polynomial $P(x)$ have degree N. Then the number of turning points for a polynomial $P(x)$ can not exceed $N-1$.

1.16 Determinants and Cramer's Rule

1. Determinant Expansions

Two by Two: $\begin{vmatrix} a & b \\ c & d \end{vmatrix} = ad - bc$

Three by Three: $\begin{vmatrix} a & b & c \\ d & e & f \\ g & h & i \end{vmatrix} = a\begin{vmatrix} e & f \\ h & i \end{vmatrix} - b\begin{vmatrix} d & f \\ g & i \end{vmatrix} + c\begin{vmatrix} d & e \\ g & h \end{vmatrix}$

2. Cramer's Rule for a Two by Two Linear System

Given $\begin{aligned} ax + by &= e \\ cx + dy &= f \end{aligned}$ with $\begin{vmatrix} a & b \\ c & d \end{vmatrix} \neq 0$

Then $x = \dfrac{\begin{vmatrix} e & b \\ f & d \end{vmatrix}}{\begin{vmatrix} a & b \\ c & d \end{vmatrix}}$ and $y = \dfrac{\begin{vmatrix} a & e \\ c & f \end{vmatrix}}{\begin{vmatrix} a & b \\ c & d \end{vmatrix}}$

4. Cramer's Rule for a Three by Three Linear System

Given $\begin{aligned} ax + by + cz &= j \\ dx + ey + fz &= k \\ gx + hy + iz &= l \end{aligned}$ with $D = \begin{vmatrix} a & b & c \\ d & e & f \\ g & h & i \end{vmatrix} \neq 0$

Then $x = \dfrac{\begin{vmatrix} j & b & c \\ k & e & f \\ l & h & i \end{vmatrix}}{D}, y = \dfrac{\begin{vmatrix} a & j & c \\ d & k & f \\ g & l & i \end{vmatrix}}{D}, z = \dfrac{\begin{vmatrix} a & b & j \\ d & e & k \\ g & h & l \end{vmatrix}}{D}$

1.17 Binomial Theorem

1. Definition of $n!$ where n is a positive integer:
$$n! = n(n-1)(n-2)...1$$

2. Special Factorials: $0! = 1$ and $1! = 1$

3. Combinatorial Symbol: $\dbinom{n}{r} = \dfrac{n!}{r!(n-r)!}$

4. Summation Symbols:
$$\sum_{i=0}^{n} a_i = a_0 + a_1 + a_2 + a_3 + a_4 + ... + a_n$$

$$\sum_{i=k}^{n} a_i = a_k + a_{k+1} + a_{k+2} + a_{k+3} ... + a_n$$

5. Binomial Theorem: $(a+b)^n = \sum_{i=0}^{n} \dbinom{n}{i} a^{n-i} b^i$

6. Sum of Binomial Coefficients when $a = b = 1$: $\sum_{i=0}^{n} \dbinom{n}{i} = 2^n$

7. Formula for $(r+1)$ st Term: $\dbinom{n}{r} a^{n-r} b^r$

8. Pascal's Triangle for $n = 10$:

```
                    1
                  1   1
                1   2   1
              1   3   3   1
            1   4   6   4   1
          1   5  10  10   5   1
        1   6  15  20  15   6   1
      1   7  21  35  35  21   7   1
    1   8  28  56  70  56  28   8   1
  1   9  36  84 126 126  84  36   9   1
1  10  45 120 210 256 210 120  45  10   1
```

25

1.18 Geometric Series

1. Definition: $\displaystyle\sum_{i=0}^{n} ar^i$ where r is the common ratio

2. Summation Formula for $\displaystyle\sum_{i=0}^{n} ar^i$: $\displaystyle\sum_{i=0}^{n} ar^i = \frac{a(1-r^{n+1})}{1-r}$

3. Summation for Infinite Number of Terms Provided $0 < r < 1$

$$\sum_{i=0}^{\infty} ar^i = \frac{a}{1-r}$$

1.19 Boolean Algebra

The propositions p & q are either True (T) or False (F).

1. Elementary Truth Table:

$and = \wedge : or = \vee : negation =\sim: implies =\Rightarrow, \Leftrightarrow$							
p	q	$\sim p$	$\sim q$	$p \wedge q$	$p \vee q$	$p \Rightarrow q$	$p \Leftrightarrow q$
T	T	F	F	T	T	T	T
T	F	F	T	F	T	F	F
F	T	T	F	F	T	F	F
F	F	T	T	T	F	T	T

2. Truth Table for Exclusive Or:

p	q	$p \overset{e}{\vee} q$
T	T	F
T	F	T
F	T	T
F	F	F

3. Modus Ponens: Let $p \Rightarrow q$ and p be True.

$\therefore q$ is True

4. Chain Rule: Let $p \Rightarrow q$ and $q \Rightarrow r$.

$\therefore p \Rightarrow r$ is True.

5. Modus Tollens: Let $p \Rightarrow q$ and q be False.

$\therefore \sim q \Rightarrow \sim p$ is True

6. Fallacy of Affirming the Consequent:

Let $p \Rightarrow q$ and q be True.

$\therefore q \Rightarrow p$ is False

7. Fallacy of Denying the Antecedent:

Let $p \Rightarrow q$ and p be False.

$\therefore \sim p \Rightarrow \sim q$ is False

8. Disjunctive Syllogism for the Exclusive Or $\overset{e}{\vee}$:

Let $p \overset{e}{\vee} q$ be True and q be False.

$\therefore p$ is True

1.20 Variation Formulas

1. Direct: $y = kx$

2. Inverse: $y = \dfrac{k}{x}$

3. Joint: $z = kxy$

4. Inverse Joint: $z = \dfrac{kx}{y}$

5. Direct to Power: $y = kx^n$

6. Inverse to Power: $y = \dfrac{k}{x^n}$

2) Geometry

2.1 Planar Areas and Perimeters

A is the planar area, P is the perimeter

   1. Square:

$$A = s^2 \text{ and } P = 4s \; ; \; s \text{ is the length of a side.}$$

   2. Rectangle:

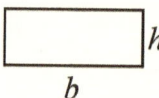

$$A = bh \text{ and } P = 2b + 2h; \; b \& h \text{ are the base and height.}$$

   3. Triangle:

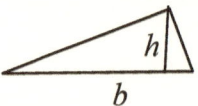

$$A = \tfrac{1}{2}bh; \; b \& h \text{ are the base and altitude.}$$

   4. Trapezoid:

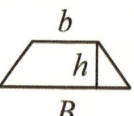

$$A = \tfrac{1}{2}(B + b)h; \; B \& b \text{ are the two parallel bases,}$$
$$\text{and } h \text{ is the altitude.}$$

5. Circle:

$$A = \pi r^2 \text{ and } P = 2\pi r \text{ ; } r \text{ is the radius.}$$

6. Ellipse:

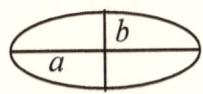

$$A = \pi ab \text{ ; } a \text{ \& } b \text{ are the half lengths of the major \& minor axes.}$$

2.2 Solid Volumes and Surface Areas

A is total surface area, V is the volume

1. Cube:

$$A = 6s^2 \text{ and } V = s^3 \text{ ; } s \text{ is the length of a side.}$$

2. Sphere:

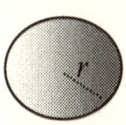

$$A = 4\pi r^2 \text{ and } V = \tfrac{4}{3}\pi r^3 \text{ ; } r \text{ is the radius.}$$

3. Cylinder:

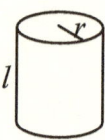

$$A = 2\pi r^2 + 2\pi r l \text{ and } V = \pi r^2 l \,;$$

r & l are the radius and length.

4. Cone:

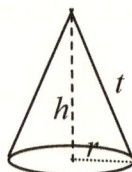

$$A = \pi r^2 + 2\pi r t \text{ and } V = \tfrac{1}{3}\pi r^2 h \,;$$

r & t & h are radius, slant height, and altitude.

5. Pyramid (square base):

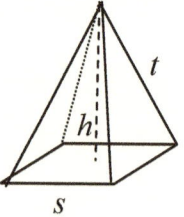

$$A = s^2 + 2st \text{ and } V = \tfrac{1}{3}s^2 h \,;$$

s & t & h are side, slant height, and altitude.

2.3 Pythagorean Theorem

Theorem Statement: Given a right triangle with one side of length x, a second side of length y, and hypotenuse of length z.

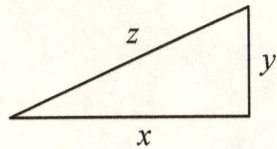

Then: $z^2 = x^2 + y^2$

1. A Traditional Algebraic Proof: Construct a big square by bringing together four congruent right triangles where each is a replicate of the triangle shown above.

$$A = (x + y)^2$$ 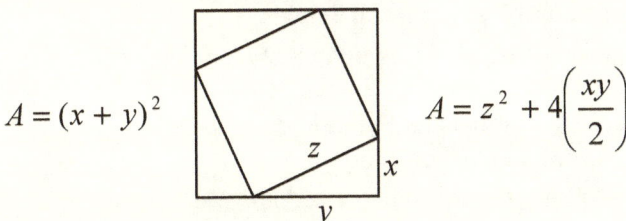 $$A = z^2 + 4\left(\frac{xy}{2}\right)$$

The area of the big square is given by

$$A = (x + y)^2 \text{, or equivalently by}$$

$$A = z^2 + 4\left(\frac{xy}{2}\right).$$

Equating:

$$(x + y)^2 = z^2 + 4\left(\frac{xy}{2}\right) \Rightarrow$$

$$x^2 + 2xy + y^2 = z^2 + 2xy \Rightarrow.$$

$$x^2 + y^2 = z^2 \Rightarrow$$

$$z^2 = x^2 + y^2 \therefore$$

2. A Pre-Algebraic Visually Intuitive Proof:

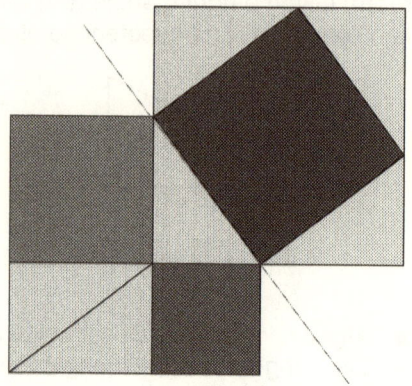

3. Definition of Pythagorean Triples:

Positive integers L, M, N such that $L^2 = M^2 + N^2$

Generating formulas for Pythagorean triples:

Let $m > n > 0$ be integers.

Then $M = m^2 - n^2 ; N = 2mn ; L = m^2 + n^2$

2.4 Heron's Formula for Triangular Area

Let $p = \frac{1}{2}(x + y + z)$ be the semi-perimeter of a general triangle

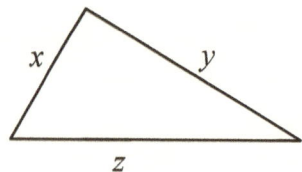

Then: $A = \sqrt{p(p - x)(p - y)(p - z)}$

32

2.5 Golden Ratio

Definition: Let $p = 1$ be the semi-perimeter of a rectangle whose base and height are in the proportion shown. This proportion defines the Golden Ratio.

$$\frac{x}{1-x} = \frac{1-x}{1}$$

Golden Ratio

Solving: $x = 0.3819$ and $1 - x = 0.6181$

2.6 Distance and Line Formulas

Let (x_1, y_1) and (x_2, y_2) be two points where $x_2 > x_1$.

1. Distance Formula: $D = \sqrt{(x_2 - x_1)^2 + (y_2 - y_1)^2}$

2. Midpoint Formula: $\left(\dfrac{x_1 + x_2}{2}, \dfrac{y_1 + y_2}{2} \right)$

3. Slope of Line: $m = \dfrac{y_2 - y_1}{x_2 - x_1}$

4. Point/Slope Form of Equation of Line: $y - y_1 = m(x - x_1)$

5. General Form of Equation of Line: $Ax + By + C = 0$

6. Slope/Intercept Form of Equation of Line: $y = mx + b$

7. Slope/Intercept Form; x and y Intercepts: $\dfrac{-b}{m}$ and b

8. Slope of Parallel Line: m

9. Slope of Line Perpendicular to a Given Line of Slope m : $\dfrac{-1}{m}$

2.7 Conic Section Formulas

1. General: $Ax^2 + Bxy + Cy^2 + Dx + Ey + f = 0$

2. Circle of Radius r Centered at (h,k):

$$(x-h)^2 + (y-k)^2 = r^2$$

3. Ellipse Centered at (h,k):

$$\frac{(x-h)^2}{a^2} + \frac{(y-k)^2}{b^2} = 1$$

If $a > b$, the two foci are on the line $y = k$ and are given by $(h-c,k)$ & $(h+c,k)$ where $c^2 = a^2 - b^2$.

If $b > a$, the two foci are on the line $x = h$ and are given by $(h,k-c)$ & $(h,k+c)$ where $c^2 = b^2 - a^2$.

4. Hyperbola Centered at (h,k):

$$\frac{(x-h)^2}{a^2} - \frac{(y-k)^2}{b^2} = 1 \text{ or}$$

$$\frac{(y-k)^2}{b^2} - \frac{(x-h)^2}{a^2} = 1$$

When $\dfrac{(x-h)^2}{a^2}$ is to the left of the minus sign,

the two foci are on the line $y = k$ and are given by $(h-c,k)$ & $(h+c,k)$ where $c^2 = a^2 + b^2$.

34

When $\dfrac{(y-k)^2}{b^2}$ is to the left of the minus sign,

the two foci are on the line $x = h$ and are given by

$(h,k-c)$ & $(h,k+c)$ where $c^2 = b^2 + a^2$.

5. Parabola with Vertex at (h,k) and Focal Length p :

$(y-k)^2 = 4p(x-h)$ or

$(x-h)^2 = 4p(y-k)$

For $(y-k)^2$, the focus is $(h+p,k)$
and the directrix is given by the line $x = h-p$.

For $(x-h)^2$, the focus is
and the directrix is given by the line $y = k-p$.

6. Transformation for removal of xy term in the general conic

$$Ax^2 + Bxy + Cy^2 + Dx + Ey + f = 0.$$

First, set $\tan(2\theta) = \dfrac{B}{A-C}$ and solve for θ.

Then, let

$$x = x'\cos\theta - y'\sin\theta$$
$$y = x'\sin\theta + y'\cos\theta$$

3) Money and Finance

P is the amount initially borrowed or deposited.
A is the total amount gained or owed.
r is the annual interest rate.
i is the annual inflation rate.
α is an annual growth rate as in the growth rate of voluntary contributions to a fund.
r_{eff} is the effective annual interest rate.
t is the time period in years for an investment.
T is the time period in years for a loan.
N is the number of compounding periods per year.
M is the monthly payment.

3.1 Simple Interest

1. Interest alone: $I = \Pr T$
2. Total repayment over T: $R = P + \Pr T = P(1 + rT)$
3. Monthly payment over T: $M = \dfrac{P(1 + rT)}{12T}$

3.2 Simple Principle Growth and Decline

1. Compounded Growth: $A = P(1 + \frac{r}{N})^{Nt}$
2. Continuous Growth: $A = Pe^{rt}$
3. Continuous Annual Inflation Rate i: $A = Pe^{-it}$

3.3 Effective Interest Rates

1. For N Compounding Periods per Year: $r_{eff} = (1 + \frac{r}{N})^{N} - 1$
2. For Continuous Interest: $r_{eff} = e^{r} - 1$

3. For a Known P, A, T: $r_{eff} = \sqrt[T]{\dfrac{A}{P}} - 1$

3.4 Continuous Interest IRA Growth Formulas

1. Annual Deposit D: $A = \dfrac{D}{r}(e^{rt} - 1)$

2. Annual Deposit D plus Initial Deposit P:

$$A = Pe^{rt} + \dfrac{D}{r}(e^{rt} - 1)$$

3. Annual Deposit D plus Initial Deposit P;
   Annual Deposit Continuously Growing via $De^{\alpha t}$:

$$A = Pe^{rt} + \dfrac{D}{r - \alpha}(e^{rt} - e^{\alpha t})$$

4. Replacement Formula: Continuous Interest to
   Compounded Interest

   Replace e^{rt} with $\left(1 + \frac{r}{N}\right)^{Nt}$

3.5 Continuous Interest Mortgage Formulas

1. First Month's Interest: $I_{1st} = \dfrac{rP}{12}$

2. Monthly Payment: $M = \dfrac{Pre^{rT}}{12(e^{rT} - 1)}$

3. Total Repayment ($P + I$): $A = \dfrac{PrTe^{rT}}{e^{rT} - 1}$

4. Total Interest Repayment: $I = P\left[\dfrac{rTe^{rT}}{e^{rT}-1}-1\right]$

5. Replacement Formula:
   Continuous Principle Reduction to
   Monthly Principle Reduction

   Replace e^{rT} with $(1+\frac{r}{12})^{12T}$

3.6 Continuous Interest Fixed-Rate Annuity Formula

Basic fact to remember: an annuity is a mortgage in reverse where the roles of the individual and financial institution have been interchanged. All continuous-interest mortgage formulas double as continuous-interest annuity formulas.

1. Monthly Annuity Payment: $M = \dfrac{Pr\,e^{rT}}{12(e^{rT}-1)}$

3.7 Markup and Markdown

$C : Cost$

$OP : Old\ \Pr ice$

$NP : New\ \Pr ice$

$P : GivenPercent(DecimalEquivalent)$

1. Markup Based on Original Cost: $NP = (1+P)C$
2. Markup Based on Cost plus New Price: $C + P \cdot NP = NP$
3. Markup Based on Old Price: $NP = (1+P)OP$
4. Markdown Based on Old Price: $NP = (1-P)OP$
5. Percent given Old and New Price: $P = NP/OP$

4) Trigonometry

4.1 Basic Definitions: Functions & Inverses

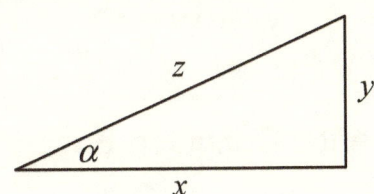

Let the figure above be a right triangle with one side of length x, a second side of length y, and a hypotenuse of length z. The angle α is opposite the side of length. The six trigonometric functions—where each is a function of α—are defined as follows:

Arbitrary z	**For** $z = 1$	**Inverse for** $z = 1$
1. $\sin(\alpha) = \dfrac{y}{z}$	$\sin(\alpha) = y$	$\sin^{-1}(y) \equiv$ $\arcsin(y) = \alpha$
2. $\cos(\alpha) = \dfrac{x}{z}$	$\cos(\alpha) = x$	$\cos^{-1}(x) \equiv$ $\arccos(x) = \alpha$
3. $\tan(\alpha) = \dfrac{y}{x}$	$\tan(\alpha) = \dfrac{y}{x}$	$\tan^{-1}\left(\frac{y}{x}\right) \equiv$ $\arctan(\frac{y}{x}) = \alpha$
4. $\cot(\alpha) = \dfrac{x}{y}$	$\cot(\alpha) = \dfrac{x}{y}$	$\cot^{-1}\left(\frac{x}{y}\right) \equiv$ $arc\cot(\frac{x}{y}) = \alpha$

5. $\sec(\alpha) = \dfrac{z}{x}$ $\qquad \sec(\alpha) = \dfrac{1}{x}$ $\qquad \begin{aligned} &\sec^{-1}(\tfrac{1}{x}) \equiv \\ &arc\sec(\tfrac{1}{x}) = \alpha \end{aligned}$

6. $\csc(\alpha) = \dfrac{z}{y}$ $\qquad \csc(\alpha) = \dfrac{1}{y}$ $\qquad \begin{aligned} &\csc^{-1}(\tfrac{1}{y}) \equiv \\ &arc\csc(\tfrac{1}{y}) = \alpha \end{aligned}$

4.2 Fundamental Definition-Based Identities

1. $\csc(\alpha) = \dfrac{1}{\sin(\alpha)}$

2. $\sec(\alpha) = \dfrac{1}{\cos(\alpha)}$

3. $\tan(\alpha) = \dfrac{\sin(\alpha)}{\cos(\alpha)}$

4. $\cot(\alpha) = \dfrac{\cos(\alpha)}{\sin(\alpha)}$

5. $\tan(\alpha) = \dfrac{1}{\cot(\alpha)}$

4.3 Pythagorean Identities

1. $\sin^2(\alpha) + \cos^2(\alpha) = 1$
2. $1 + \tan^2(\alpha) = \sec^2(\alpha)$
3. $1 + \cot^2(\alpha) = \csc^2(\alpha)$

4.4 Negative Angle Identities

1. $\sin(-\alpha) = -\sin(\alpha)$

2. $\cos(-\alpha) = \cos(\alpha)$
3. $\tan(-\alpha) = -\tan(\alpha)$
4. $\cot(-\alpha) = -\cot(\alpha)$

4.5 Sum and Difference Identities

1. $\sin(\alpha + \beta) = \sin(\alpha)\cos(\beta) + \cos(\alpha)\sin(\beta)$
2. $\sin(\alpha - \beta) = \sin(\alpha)\cos(\beta) - \cos(\alpha)\sin(\beta)$
3. $\cos(\alpha + \beta) = \cos(\alpha)\cos(\beta) - \sin(\alpha)\sin(\beta)$
4. $\cos(\alpha - \beta) = \cos(\alpha)\cos(\beta) + \sin(\alpha)\sin(\beta)$

5. $\tan(\alpha + \beta) = \dfrac{\tan(\alpha) + \tan(\beta)}{1 - \tan(\alpha)\tan(\beta)}$

6. $\tan(\alpha - \beta) = \dfrac{\tan(\alpha) - \tan(\beta)}{1 + \tan(\alpha)\tan(\beta)}$

4.6 Double Angle Identities

1. $\sin(2\alpha) = 2\sin(\alpha)\cos(\alpha)$
2. $\cos(2\alpha) = \cos^2(\alpha) - \sin^2(\alpha)$
   $\cos(2\alpha) = 2\cos^2(\alpha) - 1 = 1 - 2\sin^2(\alpha)$
3. $\tan(2\alpha) = \dfrac{2\tan(\alpha)}{1 - \tan^2(\alpha)}$

4.7 Half Angle Identities

1. $\sin\left(\dfrac{\alpha}{2}\right) = \pm\sqrt{\dfrac{1 - \cos(\alpha)}{2}}$

2. $\cos(\dfrac{\alpha}{2}) = \pm\sqrt{\dfrac{1+\cos(\alpha)}{2}}$

3. $\tan(\dfrac{\alpha}{2}) = \pm\sqrt{\dfrac{1-\cos(\alpha)}{1+\cos(\alpha)}} = \dfrac{\sin(\alpha)}{1+\cos(\alpha)} = \dfrac{1-\cos(\alpha)}{\sin(\alpha)}$

4.8 General Triangle Formulas

Applicable to all triangles: right and non-right

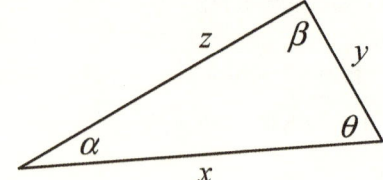

1. Sum of Interior Angles: $\alpha + \beta + \theta = 180^0$

2. Law of Sines: $\dfrac{y}{\sin(\alpha)} = \dfrac{x}{\sin(\beta)} = \dfrac{z}{\sin(\theta)}$

3. Law of Cosines:

$\quad$ a) $y^2 = x^2 + z^2 - 2xz\cos(\alpha)$
$\quad$ b) $x^2 = y^2 + z^2 - 2yz\cos(\beta)$
$\quad$ c) $z^2 = x^2 + y^2 - 2xy\cos(\theta)$

4. Area Formulas for a General Triangle:

$\quad$ a) $A = \frac{1}{2}xz\sin(\alpha)$
$\quad$ b) $A = \frac{1}{2}yz\sin(\beta)$
$\quad$ c) $A = \frac{1}{2}xy\sin(\theta)$

4.9 Arc and Sector Formulas

1. Arc Length s : $s = r\theta$
2. Area of a Sector: $A = \frac{1}{2}r^2\theta$

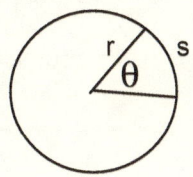

4.10 Degree/Radian Relationship

1. Basic Conversion: $180^0 = \pi$ radians
2. Conversion Formulas

From	To	Multiply by
Radians	Degrees	$\dfrac{180^0}{\pi}$
Degrees	Radians	$\dfrac{\pi}{180}$

4.11 Addition of Sine and Cosine

1. $a\sin\theta + b\cos\theta = k\sin(\theta + \alpha)$ where

$$k = \sqrt{a^2 + b^2}$$

$$\alpha = \sin^{-1}\left[\frac{b}{\sqrt{a^2 + b^2}}\right]$$

or

$$\alpha = \cos^{-1}\left[\frac{a}{\sqrt{a^2 + b^2}}\right]$$

4.12 Polar Form of Complex Numbers

1. $a + bi = r(\cos\theta + i\sin\theta)$ where

$$r = \sqrt{a^2 + b^2}, \theta = Tan^{-1}\left[\frac{b}{a}\right]$$

2. Definition of $re^{i\theta}$: $re^{i\theta} = r(\cos\theta + i\sin\theta)$

3. Euler's Famous Equality: $e^{i\pi} = -1$

4. Traditional Statement of de Moivre's Theorem:

$$[r(\cos\theta + i\sin\theta)]^n = r^n(\cos[n\theta] + i\sin[n\theta])$$

5. Alternate Statement of de Moivre's Theorem:

$$(re^{i\theta})^n = r^n e^{in\theta}$$

6. Polar Form Multiplication: $r_1 e^{i\alpha} \cdot r_2 e^{i\beta} = r_1 \cdot r_2 e^{i(\alpha+\beta)}$

7. Polar Form Division: $\dfrac{r_1 e^{i\alpha}}{r_2 e^{i\beta}} = \dfrac{r_1}{r_2} e^{i(\alpha-\beta)}$

4.13 Rectangular to Polar Coordinates

$$(x, y) \Leftrightarrow (r, \theta)$$
$$x = r\cos\theta, y = r\sin\theta$$
$$r = \sqrt{x^2 + y^2}, \theta = \tan^{-1}(x/y)$$

5) Elementary Calculus

5.1 Basic Differentiation Rules

1. Limit Definition of: $f'(x) = \lim\limits_{h \to 0} \left[\dfrac{f(x+h) - f(x)}{h} \right]$

2. Constant: $\left[k \right]' = 0$

3. Power: $\left[x^n \right]' = nx^{n-1}$, n can be <u>any exponent</u>

4. Coefficient: $\left[af(x) \right]' = af'(x)$

5. Sum/Difference: $\left[f(x) \pm g(x) \right]' = f'(x) \pm g'(x)$

6. Product: $\left[f(x)g(x) \right]' = f(x)g'(x) + g(x)f'(x)$

7. Quotient: $\left[\dfrac{f(x)}{g(x)} \right]' = \dfrac{g(x)f'(x) - f(x)g'(x)}{g(x)^2}$

8. Chain: $\left[f(g(x)) \right]' = f'(g(x))g'(x)$.

9. Inverse: $\left[f^{-1}(x) \right]' = \dfrac{1}{f'(f^{-1}(x))}$

10. Generalized Power: $\left[\{f(x)\}^n \right]' = n\{f(x)\}^{n-1} f'(x)$;

   Again, n can be <u>any exponent</u>

5.2 Transcendental Differentiation

1. $[\ln x]' = \dfrac{1}{x}$

2. $[\log_a x]' = \dfrac{1}{x \ln a}$

3. $[e^x]' = e^x$

4. $[a^x]' = a^x \ln a$

5. $[\sin x]' = \cos x$

6. $[\sin^{-1}(x)]' = \dfrac{1}{\sqrt{1-x^2}}$

7. $[\cos x]' = -\sin x$

8. $[\cos^{-1}(x)]' = \dfrac{-1}{\sqrt{1-x^2}}$

9. $[\tan x]' = \sec^2 x$

10. $[\tan^{-1}(x)]' = \dfrac{1}{1+x^2}$

11. $[\sec x]' = \sec x \tan x$

12. $[\sec^{-1}(x)]' = \dfrac{1}{|x|\sqrt{x^2-1}}$

5.3 Basic Antidifferentiation Rules

1. Constant: $\int k\,dx = kx + C$

2. Coefficient: $\int af(x)\,dx = a\int f(x)\,dx$

3. Power:

$$\int x^n\,dx = \frac{x^{n+1}}{n+1} + C, n \neq -1$$

$$\int x^{-1}\,dx = \int \frac{1}{x}\,dx = \ln|x| + C, n = -1$$

4. Sum/Difference: $\int [f(x) \pm g(x)]\,dx = \int f(x)\,dx \pm \int g(x)\,dx$

5. Parts: $\int f(x)g'(x)\,dx = f(x)g(x) - \int g(x)f'(x)\,dx$

6. Chain: $\int f'(g(x))g'(x)\,dx = f(g(x)) + C$

7. Generalized Power:

$$\int [f(x)]^n f'(x)\,dx = \frac{[f(x)]^{n+1}}{n+1} + C, n \neq -1$$

$$\int \frac{f'(x)}{f(x)}\,dx = \ln|f(x)| + C, n = -1$$

5.4 Transcendental Antidifferentiation

1. $\int \ln x \, dx = x \ln x - x + C$

2. $\int e^x \, dx = e^x + C$

3. $\int a^x \, dx = \dfrac{a^x}{\ln a} + C$

5. $\int \cos x \, dx = \sin x + C$

6. $\int \sin x \, dx = -\cos x + C$

7. $\int \tan x \, dx = \ln | \cos x | + C$

8. $\int \sec x \, dx = \ln | \sec x + \tan x | + C$

9. $\int \sec x \tan x \, dx = \sec x + C$

10. $\int \sec^2 x \, dx = \tan x + C$

11. $\int \dfrac{dx}{\sqrt{a^2 - x^2}} = \sin^{-1}\left(\dfrac{x}{a}\right) + C$

12. $\int \dfrac{dx}{a^2 + x^2} = \dfrac{1}{a} \tan^{-1}\left(\dfrac{x}{a}\right) + C$

13. $\int \dfrac{dx}{a^2 - x^2} = \dfrac{1}{2a} \ln\left| \dfrac{x-a}{x+a} \right| + C$

5.5 Lines and Approximation

1. Tangent Line at $(a, f(a))$: $y - f(a) = f'(a)(x - a)$

2. Normal Line at $(a, f(a))$: $y - f(a) = \dfrac{-1}{f'(a)}(x - a)$

3. Linear Approximation: $f(x) \cong f(a) + f'(a)(x - a)$

4. Second Order Approximation:

$$f(x) \cong f(a) + f'(a)(x - a) + \frac{f''(a)}{2}(x - a)^2$$

5. Newton's Iterative Root-Approximation Formula:

$$x_{n+1} = x_n - \frac{f(x_n)}{f'(x_n)}$$

5.6 The Fundamental Theorem of Calculus

Consider the definite integral $\displaystyle\int_a^b f(x)dx$, which can be thought of as a continuous addition process on the interval $[a, b]$, a process that sums millions upon millions of tiny quantities having the general form $f(x)dx$ from $x = a$ to $x = b$. Now, let $F(x)$ be any antiderivative for $f(x)$ where, by definition, we have that $F'(x) = f(x)$. Then, the summation process $\displaystyle\int_a^b f(x)dx$ can be evaluated by the alternative process

$$\int_a^b f(x)dx = F(x)\,|_a^b = F(b) - F(a).$$

49

6) Elementary Vector Algebra

6.1 Basic Definitions and Properties

Let $\vec{V} =< v_1, v_2, v_3 >$, $\vec{U} =< u_1, u_2, u_3 >$

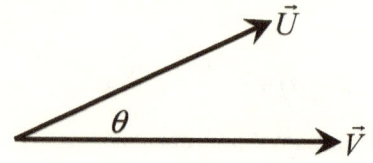

1. $\vec{U} \pm \vec{V} =< u_1 \pm v_1, u_2 \pm v_2, u_3 \pm v_3 >$
2. $(\alpha)\vec{U} =< \alpha u_1, \alpha u_2, \alpha u_3 >$
3. $-\vec{U} = (-1)\vec{U}$
4. $\vec{0} = (0,0,0)$
5. $[\vec{U}] = \sqrt{u_1^2 + u_2^2 + u_3^2}$

6. Unit Vector Parallel to $\vec{V}$: $\dfrac{1}{[\vec{V}]}\vec{V}$

7. Two Parallel Vectors: $\vec{V} \| \vec{U} \Rightarrow \exists c, st \, \vec{V} = (c)\vec{U}$

6.2 Dot Products

1. Definition of Dot Product: $\vec{U} \bullet \vec{V} = u_1 v_1 + u_2 v_2 + u_3 v_3$

2. Angle θ : $\cos \theta = \dfrac{\vec{U} \bullet \vec{V}}{[\vec{U}][\vec{V}]}$

3. Orthogonal Vectors: $\vec{U} \bullet \vec{V} = 0$

4. Projection of $\vec{U}$ onto $\vec{V}$:

$$proj_{\vec{V}}(\vec{U}) = \left[\frac{\vec{U} \bullet \vec{V}}{[\vec{V}]^2} \right] \vec{V} = \left[\frac{\vec{U} \bullet \vec{V}}{[\vec{V}]} \right] \frac{\vec{V}}{[\vec{V}]} =$$

$$[[\vec{U}] \cos \theta] \frac{\vec{V}}{[\vec{V}]}$$

6.3 Cross Products

1. Definition of Cross Product: $\vec{U} \times \vec{V} = \begin{vmatrix} i & j & k \\ u_1 & u_2 & u_3 \\ v_1 & v_2 & v_3 \end{vmatrix}$

2. Orientation of $\vec{U} \times \vec{V}$; Orthogonal to Both $\vec{U}$ and $\vec{V}$:

$$\vec{U} \bullet (\vec{U} \times \vec{V}) = \vec{V} \bullet (\vec{U} \times \vec{V}) = 0$$

3. Area of Parallelogram

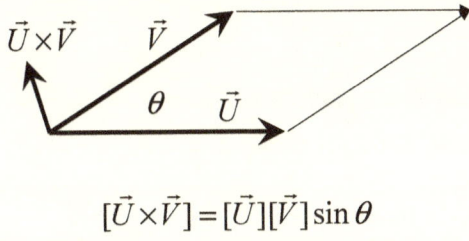

$$[\vec{U} \times \vec{V}] = [\vec{U}][\vec{V}] \sin \theta$$

51

4. Interpretation of the Triple Scalar Product:

$$\vec{U} \bullet (\vec{V} \times \vec{W}) = \begin{vmatrix} u_1 & u_2 & u_3 \\ v_1 & v_2 & v_3 \\ w_1 & w_2 & w_3 \end{vmatrix}$$

The triple scalar product is numerically equal to the volume of the parallelepiped below.

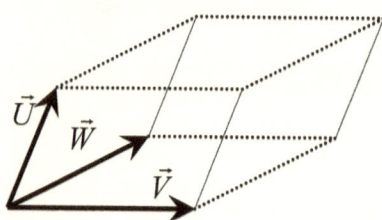

6.4 Line and Plane Equations

1. Line parallel to $<a, b, c>$ and
   Passing Through (x_1, y_1, z_1).

   If (x, y, z) is a point on the line, then:

   $$\frac{x - x_1}{a} = \frac{y - y_1}{b} = \frac{z - z_1}{c}$$

2. Equation of Plane Normal to $<a, b, c>$ and
   Passing Through (x_1, y_1, z_1).

   If (x, y, z) is a point on the plane, then:

   $$<a, b, c> \bullet <x - x_1, y - y_1, z - z_1> = 0.$$

3. Distance D between a point & plane:

If a point is given by (x_0, y_0, z_0)
and $ax + by + cz + d = 0$ is a plane, then

$$D = \frac{|ax_0 + by_0 + cz_0 + d|}{\sqrt{a^2 + b^2 + c^2}}$$

6.5 Miscellaneous Vector Equations

1. The Three Direction Cosines:

$$\cos \alpha = \frac{v_1}{[\vec{V}]}, \cos \beta = \frac{v_2}{[\vec{V}]}, \cos \gamma = \frac{v_3}{[\vec{V}]},$$

2. Definition of Work: constant force $\vec{F}$ along the path $P\vec{Q}$

$$W = \vec{F} \bullet P\vec{Q} = [proj_{P\vec{Q}}(\vec{F})][P\vec{Q}]$$

7) Probability and Statistics

7.1 Probability Formulas

Let U be a universal set consisting of all possible events.
Let Φ be the empty set consisting of no event.
Let $A, B \subset U$

1. Basic Formula: $P = \dfrac{favorable - number - of - ways}{total - number - of - ways}$

2. Fundamental Properties:
$$P(U) = 1$$
$$P(\Phi) = 0$$

3. Order Relationship: $A \subset U \Rightarrow 0 \leq P(A) \leq 1$

4. Complement Law: $P(A) = 1 - P(\sim A)$

5. Addition Law: $P(A \cup B) = P(A) + P(B) - P(A \cap B)$

6. Conditional Probability Law:
$$P(A \mid B) = \dfrac{P(A \cap B)}{P(B)}$$
$$P(B \mid A) = \dfrac{P(A \cap B)}{P(A)}$$

7. General Multiplication Law:
$$P(A \cap B) = P(B) \cdot P(A \mid B)$$
$$P(A \cap B) = P(A) \cdot P(B \mid A)$$

8. Independent Events (IE): $A \cap B = \Phi$

9. Multiplication Law for IE: $P(A \cap B) = P(A) \cdot P(B)$

7.2 Basic Concepts of Statistics

1. A **set** is an aggregate of individual items—animate or inanimate.
2. An **element** of the set is a particular item in the set.
3. An **observation** associated with the element is any attribute of interest.
4. A **statistic** associated with the element is any measurement of interest. Any statistic is an observation, but not all observations are statistics.
5. **Statistics**: the science of drawing conclusions from the totality of observations.
6. A **population** is the totality of elements that one wishes to study by making observations.
7. A **sample** is that population subset that one has the resources to study.
8. **Random sample**: where all population elements have equal probability of access.

Let a set consist of N elements where there has been observed one statistic of a similar nature for each element. The data set of all observed statistics is denoted by $\{x_1, x_2, x_3, ..., x_N\}$. The corresponding rank-ordered data set is a re-listing of the individual statistics $\{x_1, x_2, x_3, ..., x_N\}$ in numerical order from smallest to largest. Data sets can come from either populations or from samples. More than likely, the data set will be considered a sample and will be utilized to make predictions about a corresponding and much larger population.

7.3 Measures of Central Tendency

1. Sample Mean or Average $\bar{x}$: $\bar{x} = \frac{1}{N}\sum_{i=1}^{N} x_i$

2. Population Mean or Average μ : $\mu = \frac{1}{N}\sum_{i=1}^{N} x_i$

3. Median $\tilde{x}$: the middle value in a rank-ordered data set

Calculation Procedure: The median $\tilde{x}$ is the actual middle statistic if there is an odd number of data points. The median $\tilde{x}$ is the average of the two middle statistics if there is an even number of data points.

4. Mode M : the data value or statistic that occurs most often.

5. Multi-Modal Data Set: a data set with two or more modes

7.4 Measures of Dispersion

1. Range R : $R = x_L - x_S$ where x_L is the largest data value in the data set and x_S is the smallest data value

2. Sample Standard Deviation s : $s = \sqrt{\frac{1}{N-1} \sum_{i=1}^{N} (x_i - \bar{x})^2}$.

3. Population Standard Deviation σ : $\sigma = \sqrt{\frac{1}{N} \sum_{i=1}^{N} (x_i - \mu)^2}$.

4. Definition of Sample Variance: s^2

5. Definition of Population Variance: σ^2

6. Sample Coefficient of Variation C_{VS} : $C_{VS} = \dfrac{s}{\bar{x}}$

7. Population Coefficient of Variation C_{VP} : $C_{VP} = \dfrac{\sigma}{\mu}$

8. Z-Score for a Given Data Value x_i : $z_i = \dfrac{x_i - \bar{x}}{s}$

7.5 Sampling Distribution of the Mean

The mean $\bar{x}$ is formed from a sample of individual data points randomly selected from either an infinite or finite population. The number of data points selected is given by n. The sample is considered a Large Sample if $n \geq 30$; a Small Sample if $n < 30$.

1. Expected Value of $\bar{x}$: $E(\bar{x}) = \mu$

2. Standard Deviation of $\bar{x}$:

Infinite Population	Finite Population of Count N
$\sigma_{\bar{x}} = \dfrac{\sigma}{\sqrt{n}}$	$\sigma_{\bar{x}} = \sqrt{\dfrac{N-n}{N-1}}\,\dfrac{\sigma}{\sqrt{n}}$

3. Large Sample Z-score for $\bar{x}_i$: $z_i = \dfrac{\bar{x}_i - \mu}{\sigma / \sqrt{n}}$

   When σ is unknown, substitute s.

4. Interval Estimate of Population Mean:

Large-Sample Case	Small-Sample Case
$\bar{x} \pm z_{\frac{\alpha}{2}} \cdot \left[\dfrac{\sigma}{\sqrt{n}}\right]$	$\bar{x} \pm t_{\frac{\alpha}{2}} \cdot \left[\dfrac{s}{\sqrt{n}}\right]$

No assumption about the underlying population needs to be made in the large-sample case. In the small-sample case, the underlying population is assumed to be normal or nearly so. When σ is unknown in the large-sample case, substitute s.

5. Sampling Error E : $E = z_{\frac{\alpha}{2}} \cdot \left[\dfrac{\sigma}{\sqrt{n}}\right]$

6. Sample Size Needed for a Given Error E : $n = \left[\dfrac{z_{\frac{\alpha}{2}} \cdot \sigma}{E}\right]^2$.

7.6 Sampling Distribution of the Proportion

The proportion p is a quantity formed from a sample of individual data points randomly selected from either an infinite or finite population. The proportion can be thought of as a mean formulated from a sample where all the individual values are either zero (0) or one (1). The number of data points selected is given by n. The sample is considered a Large Sample if both $np \geq 5$ and $n(1-p) \geq 5$.

1. Expected Value of $\bar{p}$: $E(\bar{p}) = \mu$
2. Standard Deviation of $\bar{p}$:

Infinite Population	Finite Population of Count N
$\sigma_{\bar{p}} = \sqrt{\dfrac{p(1-p)}{n}}$	$\sigma_{\bar{p}} = \sqrt{\dfrac{N-n}{N-1}} \sqrt{\dfrac{p(1-p)}{n}}$

3. Interval Estimate of Population Proportion:

$$\bar{p} \pm z_{\frac{\alpha}{2}} \cdot \sqrt{\frac{\bar{p}(1-\bar{p})}{n}}$$

Use $\bar{p} = .5$ in $\sqrt{\dfrac{\bar{p}(1-\bar{p})}{n}}$ if clueless on the initial size of $\bar{p}$.

4. Sampling Error E : $E = z_{\frac{\alpha}{2}} \cdot \sqrt{\dfrac{p(1-p)}{n}}$

5. Sample Size Needed for a Given Error E : $n = \dfrac{z_{\frac{\alpha}{2}}^{2} \cdot p(1-p)}{E^2}$

Worse case for above with proportion unknown: $n = \dfrac{z_{\frac{\alpha}{2}}^{2}}{4E^2}$

Part II

Tables

1) Numerical

1.1 Properties of Integers 1 through 151

The standard order-of-operations applies.
^ is used for power raising and
* is used for multiplication.

INT.	CUMULATIVE SUM	FACTORS	SQUARE	SQUARE ROOT
1	1	1	1	1
2	3	Prime	4	1.4142
3	6	Prime	9	1.7321
4	10	2^2	16	2
5	15	Prime	25	2.2361
6	21	2*3	36	2.4494
7	28	Prime	49	2.6457
8	36	2^3	64	2.8284
9	45	3^3	81	3
10	55	2*5	100	3.1623
11	66	Prime	121	3.3166
12	78	2^2*3	144	3.4641
13	91	Prime	169	3.6056
14	105	2*7	196	3.7417
15	120	3*5	225	3.8730
16	136	2^4	256	4
17	153	Prime	289	4.1231
18	171	2*3^3	324	4.2426
19	190	Prime	361	4.3589
20	210	2^2*5	400	4.4721
21	231	3*7	441	4.5826
22	255	2*11	484	4.6904
23	278	Prime	529	4.7958
24	302	2^3*3	576	4.8990
25	327	5^5	625	5
26	351	2*13	676	5.1000

INT.	CUMULATIVE SUM	FACTORS	SQUARE	SQUARE ROOT
27	378	3^3	729	5.1962
28	406	2^2*7	784	5.2915
29	435	Prime	841	5.3852
30	465	2*3*5	900	5.4772
31	496	Prime	961	5.5678
32	528	2^5	1024	5.6568
33	561	3*11	1089	5.7446
34	595	2*17	1156	5.8310
35	630	5*7	1225	5.9161
36	666	2^2*3^2	1296	6.0000
37	703	Prime	1369	6.0828
38	741	2*19	1444	6.1644
39	780	3*13	1521	6.2445
40	820	2^3*5	1600	6.3246
41	861	Prime	1681	6.4031
42	903	2*3*7	1764	6.4807
43	946	Prime	1849	6.5574
44	990	2^2*11	1936	6.6332
45	1035	3^3*5	2025	6.7082
46	1081	2*23	2116	6.7823
47	1128	Prime	2209	6.8557
48	1176	2^4*3	2304	6.9282
49	1225	7^7	2401	7.0000
50	1275	2*5^2	2500	7.0711
51	1326	3*17	2601	7.1414
52	1378	2^2*13	2704	7.2111
53	1431	Prime	2809	7.2801
54	1485	2*3^3	2916	7.3485
55	1540	5*11	3025	7.4162
56	1596	2^3*7	3136	7.4833
57	1653	3*19	3249	7.5498
58	1711	2*29	3364	7.6158
59	1770	Prime	3481	7.6811
60	1830	2^2*3*5	3600	7.7460
61	1891	Prime	3721	7.8102

INT.	CUMULATIVE SUM	FACTORS	SQUARE	SQUARE ROOT
62	1953	2*31	3884	7.8740
63	2016	3^3*7	3969	7.9373
64	2080	2^6	4096	8.0000
65	2145	5^13	4225	8.0623
66	2211	2*3*11	4356	8.1240
67	2278	Prime	4489	8.1854
68	2346	2^2*17	4624	8.2462
69	2415	3*23	4761	8.3066
70	2485	2*5*7	4900	8.3666
71	2556	Prime	5041	8.4261
72	2628	2^3*3^2	5184	8.4852
73	2701	Prime	5329	8.5440
74	2775	2*3^3	5476	8.6023
75	2850	3*5^2	5625	8.6603
76	2926	2^2*19	5776	8.7178
77	3003	7*11	5929	8.7750
78	3081	2*3*13	6084	8.8318
79	3160	Prime	6241	8.8882
80	3240	2^4*5	6400	8.9443
81	3321	3^4	6561	9.0000
82	3403	2*41	6724	9.0554
83	3486	Prime	6889	9.1104
84	3570	2^2*3*7	7056	9.1652
85	3655	5*17	7225	9.2200
86	3741	2*43	7396	9.2736
87	3828	3*29	7569	9.3274
88	3916	2^3*11	7744	9.3808
89	4005	Prime	7921	9.4340
90	4095	2*3^2*5	8100	9.4868
91	4186	Prime	8281	9.5394
92	4278	2^2*23	8464	9.5917
93	4371	3*31	8649	9.6437
94	4465	2*47	8836	9.6954

INT.	CUMULATIVE SUM	FACTORS	SQUARE	SQUARE ROOT
95	4560	5*19	9025	9.7468
96	4656	2^5*3	9216	9.7980
97	4753	Prime	9409	9.8489
98	4851	2*7^2	9604	9.8995
99	4950	3^2*11	9801	9.9499
100	5050	2^2*5^2	10000	10.0000
101	5151	Prime	10201	10.0499
102	5253	2*3*17	10404	10.0995
103	5356	Prime	10609	10.1489
104	5460	2^3*13	10816	10.1980
105	5565	3*5*7	11025	10.2470
106	5671	2*53	11236	10.2956
107	5778	Prime	11449	10.3441
108	5886	2^2*3*3	11664	10.3923
109	5995	Prime	11881	10.4403
110	6105	2*5*11	12100	10.4881
111	6216	3*37	12321	10.5357
112	6328	2^4*7	12544	10.5830
113	6441	Prime	12769	10.6301
114	6555	2*3*19	12996	10.6771
115	6670	5*23	13225	10.7238
116	6786	2^2*29	13456	10.7703
117	6903	3^3*13	13689	10.8167
118	7021	2*59	13924	10.8628
119	7140	7*17	14161	10.9087
120	7260	2^3*3*5	14400	10.9546
121	7381	11^2	14641	11.0000
122	7503	2*61	14884	11.0454
123	7626	3*41	15129	11.0905
124	7750	2^2*31	15376	11.1355
125	7875	5^3	15625	11.1803
126	8001	2*3^2*7	15876	11.2250
127	8128	Prime	16129	11.2694

INT.	CUMULATIVE SUM	FACTORS	SQUARE	SQUARE ROOT
128	8256	2^7	16384	11.3137
129	8385	3*43	16641	11.3578
130	8515	2*5*13	16900	11.4018
131	8646	Prime	17161	11.4455
132	8778	2*61	17424	11.4891
133	8911	7*19	17689	11.5326
134	9045	2*67	17956	11.5758
135	9180	3^3*5	18225	11.6180
136	9316	2^3*17	18496	11.6619
137	9453	Prime	18769	11.7047
138	9591	2*3*23	19044	11.7473
139	9730	Prime	19321	11.7898
140	9870	2^2*5*7	19600	11.8322
141	10011	3*47	19881	11.8743
142	10153	2*71	20164	11.9164
143	10296	11*13	20449	11.9583
144	10440	2^4*3^2	20736	12.0000
145	10585	5*29	21025	12.0416
146	10731	2*73	21316	12.0830
147	10878	3*7^2	21609	12.1244
148	11026	2^2*37	21904	12.1655
149	11175	Prime	22201	12.2066
150	11325	2*3*5^2	22500	12.2474
151	11476	Prime	22801	12.2882

1.2 Nine Elementary Memory Numbers

NUM	MEM	NUM	MEM	NUM	MEM
$\sqrt{2}$	1.4142	$\sqrt{7}$	2.6457	ϕ	0.6180
$\sqrt{3}$	1.7321	π	3.1416	$\ln(10)$	2.3026
$\sqrt{5}$	2.2361	e	2.7182	$Log(e)$	0.4343

1.3 Roman Numerals

ARABIC	ROMAN	ARABIC	ROMAN	ARABIC	ROMAN
1	I	10	X	101	CI
2	II	11	XI	200	CC
3	III	15	XV	500	D
4	IV	20	XX	600	DI
5	V	30	XXX	1000	M
6	VI	40	XL	5000	V bar
7	VII	50	L	10000	L bar
8	VIII	60	LX	100000	C bar
9	IX	100	C	1000000	M bar

1.4 Prime Numbers less than 1000

Prime pairs are shown in italics. The black spaces indicate century breaks.

2	*3*	*5*	*7*	*11*	*13*	*17*	*19*	23	*29*
31	37	*41*	*43*	47	53	*59*	*61*	67	*71*
73	79	83	89	97	■	*101*	*103*	*107*	*109*
113	127	131	*137*	*139*	*149*	*151*	157	163	167
173	*179*	*181*	*191*	*193*	*197*	*199*	■	211	223
227	*229*	233	*239*	*241*	251	257	263	269	271
277	*281*	*283*	293	■	307	*311*	*313*	317	331
337	*347*	*349*	353	359	367	373	379	383	389
397	■	401	409	*419*	*421*	*431*	*433*	439	443
449	457	*461*	*463*	467	479	487	491	499	■
503	509	*521*	*523*	541	547	557	563	*569*	*571*
577	587	593	599	■	601	607	613	*617*	*619*
631	*641*	*643*	647	653	*659*	*661*	673	677	683
691	■	701	709	719	727	733	739	743	751
757	761	769	773	787	797	■	*809*	*811*	*821*
823	*827*	*829*	839	853	857	859	863	877	*881*
883	887	■	907	911	919	929	937	941	947
953	967	971	977	983	991	997	■	■	■

1.5 Twelve-by-Twelve Multiplication Table

Different font sizes are used for, one, two, or three-digit entries.

×	1	2	3	4	5	6	7	8	9	10	11	12
1	1	2	3	4	5	6	7	8	9	10	11	12
2	2	4	6	8	10	12	14	16	18	20	22	24
3	3	6	9	12	15	18	21	24	27	30	33	36
4	4	8	12	16	20	24	28	32	36	40	44	48
5	5	10	15	20	25	30	35	40	45	50	55	60
6	6	12	18	24	30	36	42	48	54	60	66	72
7	7	14	21	28	35	42	49	56	63	70	77	84
8	8	16	24	32	40	48	56	64	72	80	88	96
9	9	18	27	36	45	54	63	72	81	90	99	108
10	10	20	30	40	50	60	70	80	90	100	110	120
11	11	22	33	44	55	66	77	88	99	110	121	132
12	12	24	36	48	60	72	84	96	108	120	132	144

1.6 American Names for Large Numbers

NUM	NAME	NUM	NAME	NUM	NAME
10^3	thousand	10^18	quintillion	10^33	decillion
10^6	million	10^21	sextillion	10^36	undecillion
10^9	billion	10^24	septillion	10^39	duodecillion
10^12	trillion	10^27	octillion	10^48	quidecillion
10^15	quadrillion	10^30	nontillion	10^63	vigintillion

1.7 The Random Digits of PI

The digits of PI pass every randomness test.
Hence, the first 900 serve double duty
as a random number table

PI=3.-- READ LEFT TO RIGHT, TOP TO BOTTOM					
14159	26535	89793	23846	26433	83279
50288	41971	69399	37510	58209	74944
59230	78164	06286	20899	86280	34825
34211	70679	82148	08651	32823	06647
09384	46095	50582	23172	53594	08128
48111	74502	84102	70193	85211	05559
64462	29489	54930	38196	44288	10975
66593	34461	28475	64823	37867	83165
27120	19091	45648	56692	34603	48610
45432	66482	13393	60726	02491	41273
72458	70066	06315	58817	48815	20920
96282	92540	91715	36436	78925	90360
01133	05305	48820	46652	13841	46951
94151	16094	33057	27036	57595	91953
09218	61173	81932	61179	31051	18548
07446	23799	62749	56735	18857	52724
89122	79381	83011	94912	98336	73362
44065	66430	86021	39494	63952	24737
19070	21798	60943	70277	05392	17176
29317	67523	84674	81846	76694	05132
00056	81271	45263	56052	77857	71342
75778	96091	73637	17872	14684	40901
22495	34301	46549	58537	10507	92279
68925	89235	42019	95611	21290	21960
86403	44181	59813	62977	47713	09960
51870	72113	49999	99837	29784	49951
05973	17328	16096	31859	50244	59455
34690	83026	42522	30825	33446	85035
26193	11881	71010	00313	78387	52886
58753	32083	81420	61717	76691	47303

1.8 Standard Normal Distribution

THE STANDARD NORMAL DISTRIBUTION: TABLE VALUES ARE THE RIGHT TAIL AREA FOR A GIVEN Z									
Z	0.00	0.01	0.02	0.03	0.04	0.05	0.06	0.07	0.08	0.09
0.0	.5000	.4960	.4920	.4880	.4840	.4800	.4761	.4761	.4681	.4641
0.1	.4602	.4562	.4522	.4483	.4443	.4404	.4364	.4325	.4286	.4247
0.2	.4207	.4168	.4129	.4090	.4051	.4013	.3974	.3936	.3897	.3858
0.3	.3821	.3783	.3744	.3707	.3669	.3631	.3594	.3556	.3520	.3483
0.4	.3446	.3409	.3372	.3336	.3300	.3263	.3228	.3192	.3156	.3121
0.5	.3085	.3050	.3015	.2980	.2946	.2911	.2877	.2843	.2809	.2776
0.6	.2742	.2709	.2676	.2643	.2611	.2578	.2546	.2514	.2482	.2451
0.7	.2420	.2389	.2358	.2327	.2297	.2266	.2236	.2206	.2176	.2148
0.8	.2119	.2090	.2061	.2033	.2005	.1977	.1949	.1922	.1894	.1867
0.9	.1841	.1814	.1788	.1761	.1736	.1711	.1685	.1660	.1635	.1611
1.0	.1587	.1562	.1539	.1515	.1492	.1469	.1446	.1423	.1401	.1379
1.1	.1357	.1335	.1314	.1292	.1271	.1250	.1230	.1210	.1190	.1170
1.2	.1151	.1131	.1112	.1093	.1074	.1056	.1038	.1020	.1003	.0985
1.3	.0968	.0951	.0934	.0918	.0901	.0885	.0869	.0853	.0837	.0822
1.4	.0807	.0793	.0778	.0764	.0749	.0735	.0721	.0708	.0694	.0681
1.5	.0668	.0655	.0642	.0630	.0618	.0606	.0594	.0582	.0570	.0559
1.6	.0548	.0536	.0526	.0515	.0505	.0495	.0485	.0475	.0465	.0455
1.7	.0445	.0436	.0427	.0418	.0409	.0401	.0392	.0384	.0375	.0367
1.8	.0359	.0351	.0344	.0336	.0329	.0322	.0314	.0307	.0301	.0294
1.9	.0287	.0280	.0274	.0268	.0262	.0255	.0250	.0244	.0238	.0232
2.0	.0228	.0222	.0217	.0212	.0206	.0202	.0197	.0192	.0187	.0183
2.1	.0178	.0174	.0170	.0165	.0162	.0158	.0154	.0150	.0146	.0143
2.2	.0139	.0136	.0132	.0128	.0125	.0122	.0119	.0116	.0113	.0110
2.3	.0107	.0104	.0101	.0099	.0096	.0094	.0091	.0089	.0087	.0084
2.4	.0082	.0080	.0078	.0075	.0073	.0071	.0069	.0068	.0066	.0064
2.5	.0062	.0060	.0058	.0057	.0055	.0054	.0052	.0050	.0049	.0048
2.6	.0047	.0045	.0044	.0043	.0041	.0040	.0039	.0038	.0037	.0036
2.7	.0035	.0034	.0033	.0032	.0031	.0030	.0029	.0028	.0027	.0026
2.8	.0026	.0025	.0024	.0023	.0023	.0022	.0021	.0020	.0020	.0019
2.9	.0019	.0018	.0018	.0017	.0016	.0016	.0015	.0015	.0014	.0014
3.0	.0013	.0013	.0013	.0012	.0012	.0011	.0011	.0011	.0010	.0010
3.1	.0010	.0010	.0009	.0009	.0009	.0009	.0009	.0008	.0008	.0008
3.2	.0007	.0007	.0006	.0007	.0007	.0006	.0006	.0005	.0005	.0005
3.3	.0005	.0005	.0005	.0004	.0004	.0004	.0004	.0004	.0004	.0004
3.4	.0003	.0003	.0003	.0003	.0003	.0003	.0003	.0003	.0003	.0002
3.5	.0002	.0002	.0002	.0002	.0002	.0002	.0002	.0002	.0002	.0002
3.6	.0002	.0002	.0002	.0001	.0001	.0001	.0001	.0001	.0001	.0001
3.7	.0001	.0001	.0001	Right Tail Area starts to fall below 0.0001						

1.8 Two-Sided Student's t Statistic

TABLE VALUES ARE T SCORES NEEDED TO GUARANTEE THE PERCENT CONFIDENCE			
Degrees of freedom: DF	90%	95%	99%
1	6.314	12.706	63.657
2	2.920	4.303	9.925
3	2.353	3.182	5.841
4	2.132	2.776	4.604
5	2.015	2.571	4.032
6	1.943	2.447	3.707
7	1.895	2.365	3.499
8	1.860	2.306	3.355
9	1.833	2.262	3.250
10	1.812	2.228	3.169
11	1.796	2.201	3.106
12	1.782	2.179	3.055
13	1.771	2.160	3.012
14	1.761	2.145	2.977
15	1.753	2.131	2.947
16	1.746	2.120	2.921
17	1.740	2.110	2.898
18	1.734	2.101	2.878
19	1.729	2.093	2.861
20	1.725	2.083	2.845
21	1.721	2.080	2.831
22	1.717	2.074	2.819
23	1.714	2.069	2.907
24	1.711	2.064	2.797
25	1.708	2.060	2.787
26	1.706	2.056	2.779
27	1.703	2.052	2.771
28	1.701	2.048	2.763
29	1.699	2.045	2.756
30	1.697	2.042	2.750
40	1.684	2.021	2.704
60	1.671	2.000	2.660
120	1.658	1.980	2.617
∞	1.645	1.960	2.576

1.9 Date and Day of Year

DATE	DAY	DATE	DAY	DATE	DAY
Jan 1	1	May 1	121	Sep 1	244
Jan 5	5	May 5	125	Sep 5	248
Jan 8	8	May 8	128	Sep 8	251
Jan 12	12	May 12	132	Sep 12	255
Jan 15	15	May 15	135	Sep 15	258
Jan 19	19	May 19	139	Sep 19	262
Jan 22	22	May 22	142	Sep 22	265
Jan 26	26	May 26	146	Sep 26	269
Feb 1	32	Jun 1	152	Oct 1	274
Feb 5	36	Jun 5	156	Oct 6	278
Feb 8	39	Jun 8	159	Oct 8	281
Feb 12	43	Jun 12	163	Oct 12	285
Feb 15	46	Jun 15	166	Oct 15	288
Feb 19	50	Jun 19	170	Oct 19	292
Feb 22	53	Jun 22	173	Oct 22	295
Feb 26	57	Jun 26	177	Oct 26	299
Mar 1	60**	Jul 1	182	Nov 1	305
Mar 5	64	Jul 5	186	Nov 5	309
Mar 8	67	Jul 8	189	Nov 8	312
Mar 12	71	Jul 12	193	Nov 12	316
Mar 15	74	Jul 15	196	Nov 15	319
Mar 19	78	Jul 19	200	Nov 19	323
Mar 22	81	Jul 22	203	Nov 22	326
Mar 26	85	Jul 26	207	Nov 26	330
Apr 1	91	Aug 1	213	Dec1	335
Apr 5	96	Aug 5	218	Dec 5	339
Apr 8	98	Aug 8	220	Dec 8	342
Apr 12	102	Aug 12	224	Dec 12	346
Apr 15	105	Aug 15	227	Dec 15	349
Apr 19	109	Aug 19	331	Dec 19	353
Apr 22	112	Aug 22	234	Dec 22	356
Apr 26	116	Aug 26	238	Dec 26	360
** Add one day starting here if a leap year					

2) Physical Sciences

2.1 Conversion Factors in Allied Health

General comments:

1. All three systems—apothecary, household and metric Systems—have rough volume equivalents.
2. Since the household system is a volume-only system, the Weight Exchange Table does not include household equivalents.
3. Common discrepancies that are still considered correct are shown in *italics*.

Volume Conversion Table

Apothecary		Household		Metric
1minim		1drop	1gtt	
16minims				1mL (cc)
60minims	1fluidram	60gtts	1tsp	5mL (cc) *or 4mL*
4fluidrams	0.5fluidounce	3tsp	1tbsp	15mL (cc)
8fluidrams	1fluidounce	2tbsp		30mL (cc)
	8fluidounces	1cup		240mL (cc)
	16fluidounces	2cups	1pint	500mL (cc) *or 480mL*
	32fluidounces	2pints	1quart	1000mL (cc) *or 960mL*

Weight Conversion Table

Apothecary		Metric
1grain		60mg *or 64mg*
15grains		1g
60grains	1dram	4g
8drams	1ounce	32g
12ounces	1pound	384g

2.2 Medical Abbreviations in Allied Health

ABBREVIATION	MEANING
b.i.d.	Twice a day
b.i.w.	Twice a week
c	With
cap, caps	Capsule
dil.	Dilute
DS	Double strength
gtt	Drop
h, hr	Hour
h.s.	Hour of sleep, at bedtime
I.M.	Intramuscular
I.V.	Intravenous
n.p.o., NPO	Nothing by mouth
NS, N/S	Normal saline
o.d.	Once a day, every day
p.o	By or through mouth
p.r.n.	As needed, as necessary
q.	Every, each
q.a.m.	Every morning
q.d.	Every day
q.h.	Every hour
q2h	Every two hours
q4h	Every four hours
q.i.d.	Four times a day
ss	One half
s.c., S.C., s.q.	Subcutaneous
stat, STAT	Immediately, at once
susp	Suspension
tab	Tablet
t.i.d.	Three times a day
P% strength	P grams per 100 mL
A:B strength	A grams per B mL

2.3 Wind Chill Table

Grey area is the danger zone where exposed human flesh will begin to freeze within one minute.

		WIND SPEED (mph)							
		5	10	15	20	25	30	35	40
	35	31	27	25	24	23	22	21	20
	30	25	21	19	17	16	15	14	13
	25	19	15	13	11	9	8	7	6
T	20	13	9	6	4	3	1	0	-1
E	15	7	3	0	-2	-4	-5	-7	-8
M	10	1	-4	-7	-9	-11	-12	-14	-15
P	5	-5	-10	-13	-15	-17	-19	-21	-22
	0	-11	-16	-19	-22	-24	-26	-27	-29
°F	-5	-16	-22	-26	-29	-31	-33	-34	-36
	-10	-22	-28	-32	-35	-37	-39	-41	-43
	-15	-28	-35	-39	-42	-44	-46	-48	-50
	-20	-34	-41	-45	-48	-51	-53	-55	-57
	-25	-40	-47	-51	-55	-58	-60	-62	-64

2.4 Heat Index Table

The number in the body of the table is the equivalent heating temperature at 0% humidity

		RELATIVE HUMIDITY (%)							
		30	40	50	60	70	80	85	90
T	105	114	123	135	148	163	180	190	199
E	104	112	121	131	144	158	175	184	193
M	103	110	118	128	140	154	169	178	186
P	102	108	116	125	136	149	164	172	180
	101	106	113	122	133	145	159	166	174
°F	100	104	111	119	129	141	154	161	168
	97	99	105	112	120	129	140	145	152
	95	96	101	107	114	122	131	136	141
	90	89	92	96	100	106	112	115	119

2.5 Temperature Conversion Formulas

Fahrenheit to Celsius: $C = \dfrac{F - 32}{1.8}$

Celsius to Fahrenheit: $F = 1.8C + 32$

2.6 Master Unit Conversion Table

Arranged in alphabetical order

TO CONVERT	TO	MULTIPLY BY
acres	ft^2	43560
acres	m^2	4046.9
acres	rods	160
acres	hectares	0.4047
acre feet	barrels	7758
acre feet	m^3	1233.5
Angstrom (å)	cm	10E-8
Angstrom	nm	0.1
astronomical unit (AU)	cm	1.496E13
astronomical unit	km	1.496E8
atmospheres (atm)	feet H2O	33.94
atmospheres	in of Hg	29.92
atmospheres	mm of Hg	760
atmospheres	psi	14.7
bar	atm	.98692
bar	$dyne/cm^2$	10E6
bar	psi (lb/in^2)	14.5038
bar	mm Hg	750.06
bar	MPa	10E-1
barrels (bbl)	ft^3	5.6146
barrels	m^3	0.15898
barrels	gal (US)	42
barrels	liter	158.9

TO CONVERT	TO	MULTIPLY BY
BTU	Canadian BTU	1.000418022
BTU	cal	251.996
BTU	erg	1.055055853 E-10
BTU	joule	1054.35
calorie (cal)	joule	4.184
centimeter (cm)	inch	0.39370
cm	m	1E-2
darcy	m^2	9.8697E-13
dyne	$g\ cm\ /s^2$	1
dyne	Newton	10E-5
erg	cal	2.39006E-8
erg	dyne cm	1
erg	joule	10E-7
fathom	ft	6
feet (ft)	in	12
feet	m	0.3048
furlong	yd	220
gallon (US gal)	in^3	231
gallon	liter	3.78541
(Imperial) gal	in^3	277.419
gallon	liter	4.54608
gamma	Gauss	10E-5
gamma	Tesla	10E-9
gauss	Tesla	10E-4
gram (g)	pound	0.0022046
gram	kg	10E-3
hectare	acre	2.47105
hectare	cm^2	10E-8
horsepower	Watt (W)	745.700

TO CONVERT	TO	MULTIPLY BY
inch (in)	cm	2.54
inch (in)	mm	25.4
joule (J)	erg	10E7
joule	cal	0.239006
kilogram (kg)	g	10E3
kilogram	pound	2.20462
kilometer (km)	m	10E3
kilometer	ft	3280.84
kilometer	mile	0.621371
Kilometer/hr (kph)	mile/hr (mph)	0.621371
kilowatt	hp	1.34102
knot	mph	1.150779
liter	cm^3	10E3
liter	gal (US)	0.26417
liter	in^3	61.0237
meter	angstrom	10E10
meter	ft	3.28084
micron	cm	10E-4
mile	ft	5280
mile	km	1.60934
mm Hg	$dyne/cm^2$	1333.22
Newton	dyne	10E5
Newton	pound force	0.224809
Newton-meter (torque)	foot-pound-force	0.737562
ounce	lb	0.0625
Pascal	atmospheres	9.86923 x10E-6
Pascal	psi	1.45 x10E-4
Pascal	torr	7.501 x10E-3
pint	gallon	0.125
poise	g /cm/s	1
poise	kg /m/s	0.1

TO CONVERT	TO	MULTIPLY BY
pound mass	kg	0.453592
pound force	Newton	4.4475
rod	feet	16.5
quart	gallon	0.25
stoke	cm^2 /s	1
slug	kg	14.594
Tesla	Gauss	10E4
Torr	millibar	1.333224
Torr	millimeter hg	1
ton (long)	lb	2240
ton (metric)	lb	2205
ton (metric)	kg	1000
ton (short or net)	lb	2000
ton (short or net)	kg	907.185
ton (short or net)	ton (metric)	0.907
watt	J /s	1
yard	in	36
yard	m	0.9144
year (calendar)	days	365.242198781
year (calendar)	s	3.15576 x 10E7

2.7 Properties of Earth and Moon

PROPERTY	VALUE	PROPERTY	VALUE
Distance from sun	9.2.9x10^6 miles	Earth Surface g	32.2 ft/s^2
Equatorial diameter	7926 miles	Moon distance from earth	238,393 miles
Length of day	24 hours	Moon diameter	2160 miles
Length of year	365.26 days	Moon revolution	27 days, 7 hours

2.8 Metric System

Basic and Derived Units

QUANTITY	NAME	SYMBOL	UNITS
Length	meter	m	*basic unit*
Time	second	s	*basic unit*
Mass	kilogram	kg	*basic unit*
Temperature	Kelvin	K	*basic unit*
Electrical Current	ampere	A	*basic unit*
Force	Newton	N	$kg\ m\ s^{-2}$
Volume	Liter	L	m^3
Energy	joule	J	$kg\ m^2\ s^{-2}$
Power	watt	W	$kg\ m^2\ s^{-3}$
Frequency	hertz	Hz	s^{-1}
Charge	coulomb	C	$A\ s$
Capacitance	farad	F	$C^2\ s^2\ kg^{-1}\ m^{-2}$
Magnetic Induction	Tesla	T	$kg\ A^{-1}\ s^{-2}$

Metric Prefixes

PREFIX	FACTOR	SYMBOL	METER EXAMPLE
peta	10^15	E	Em
tera	10^12	P	Pm
giga	10^9	G	Gm
mega	10^6	M	Mm
kilo	10^3	k	km
hecto	10^2	h	hm
deca	10^1	da	dam
deci	10^(-1)	d	dm
centi	10^(-2)	c	cm
milli	10^(-3)	m	mm
micro	10^(-6)	μ	μm
nano	10^(-9)	n	nm
pica	10^(-12)	p	pm

2.9 British System

Basic and Derived Units

QUANTITY	NAME	SYMBOL	UNITS
Length	foot	ft	*basic unit*
Time	second	s	*basic unit*
Mass	slug		*basic unit*
Temperature	Fahrenheit	^{0}F	*basic unit*
Electrical Current	ampere	A	*basic unit*
Force	pound	lb	*derived unit*
Volume	gallon	gal	*derived unit*
Work	foot-pound	ft-lb	*derived unit*
Power	horsepower	hp	*derived unit*
Charge	coulomb	C	*derived unit*
Capacitance	farad	F	*derived unit*
Heat	British thermal unit	Btu	*basic unit*

Uncommon British Measures

WEIGHT	LINEAR
Grain=Basic Unit	**Inch=Basic Unit**
1 scruple=20 grains	1 hand=4 inches
1 dram=3 scruples	1 link=7.92 inches
1 ounce=16 drams	1 span=9 inches
1 pound=16 ounces	1 foot=12 inches
1 hundredweight=100 pounds	1 yard=3 feet
1 ton=2000 pounds	1 fathom=2 yards
1 long ton=2240 pounds	1 rod=5.5 yards
	1 chain=100 links=22 yards
	1 furlong=220 yards
	1 mile=1760 yards
	1 knot mile=6076.1155 feet
	1 league=3 miles

Uncommon British Measures (continued)

LIQUID	DRY
Gill=Basic Unit	Pint=Basic Unit
1 pint=4 gills	1 quart=2 pints
1 quart= 2 pints	1 gallon=4 quarts
1 gallon=4 quarts	1 peck=2 gallons
1 hogshead=63 gallons	1 bushel=4 pecks
1 pipe (or butt)=2 hogsheads	
1 tun=2 pipes	

Miscellaneous Measures

AREA	ASTRONOMY
1 square chain=16 square rods	1 astronomical unit (AU) = 93,000,000 miles
1 acre=43,560 square feet	1 light second = 186,000 miles =0.002 AU
1 acre=160 square rods	1 light year = 5.88×10^{12} miles =6.3226×10^{4} AU
1 square mile = 640 square acres	1 parsec (pc) = 3.26 light years
1 square mile = 1 section	1 kpc=1000pc
1 township = 36 sections	1 mpc = 1000000pc

VOLUME
1 U.S. liquid gallon= 231 cubic inches
I Imperial gallon=1.2 U.S. gallons=0.16 cubic feet
1 cord=128 cubic feet

Part III

Puzzles and Curios

1) Puzzles

1.1 The Old Glory Puzzle

September 11, 2001 is a date that we baby boomers will remember in much the same fashion that our parents remembered December 7, 1941. Our flag is once again enjoying a newfound popularity! Early baby boomers, such as myself, were born under a forty-eight star flag. This flag was arranged in six rows of eight stars each. Hawaii joined the Union in 1959, leading to a forty-nine star flag—seven rows of seven stars each. Alaska joined the Union one year later, leading to the present fifty star flag arranged in nine slightly nested rows alternating seven, six, seven, six, seven, six, seven, six, and seven stars.

Suppose new states are added to the Union during the current century. Possibilities might include Puerto Rico, Guam, and the District of Columbia.

Challenge: Arrange three rectangular fields to accommodate fifty-one, fifty-two, and fifty-three stars. Use the dual constraint that there shall be no more than nine rows and no more than eight stars per row, a historical precedent. Having problems? Step away from the rectangular pattern—literally, out-of-the-box thinking—and go to a circular pattern, utilized at least once in our nation's history.

Finally, for those of you who need even more of a challenge, keep on adding the states and stars all the way to seventy-two—nine times eight.

1.2 Two Squares and Two Challenges

The following two puzzles have been used as icebreakers for years in various group settings. Both are simple yet profound and illustrate the use of out-of-the-box or lateral thinking.

1) Try to connect all nine dots using just four straight-line segments and one continuous pen stroke.

2) Count the total number of squares contained in the big square below.

1.3 Crossing Problems Old and New

Logic problems where several animals, objects, and/or people must cross over a river under a set of constraints have entertained and baffled puzzle solvers for many centuries. Below are two such problems. The first is at least 1000 years old, and urban legend has it that the second was a question on a Microsoft employment exam. Enjoy the two challenges!

Wolf, Goat, and Cabbage

A farmer and his goat, wolf, and cabbage come to a river that they wish to cross. There is a boat, but it only has room for two, and the farmer is the only one who can row. However, if the farmer leaves the shore in order to row, the goat will eat the cabbage, and the wolf will eat the goat.

Challenge: Devise a minimum number of crossings so that all concerned make it across the river alive and in one piece.

The "U2" Concert

"U2", the four-man Irish rock band, has a concert that starts in 17 minutes, and they all must cross a bridge in order to get there. All four men begin on the same side of the bridge. Your job is to devise a plan to help the group get to the other side on time. There are several constraints that complicate the crossing process: It is night and a flashlight must be used, but there is only one flashlight available. Any party that crosses—only 1 or 2 people allowed on the bridge at any given time—must have the flashlight with them. The flashlight must be walked back and forth; it cannot be thrown, teleported, etc. Each band member walks at a different speed, and a pair walking together must cross the bridge using the slower man's speed. Here are the four crossing times: Bono takes 1 minute to cross; Edge, 2 minutes to cross; Adam, 5 minutes to cross; and Larry, 10 minutes to cross.

Challenge: Devise the plan!

1.4 The Camel and the Bananas

A camel used to transport bananas must travel 1000 miles across a desert to reach customers living in an exotic city. At any given time, the camel can carry up to 1000 bananas and must eat one banana for every mile it walks.

Challenge: Assuming an initial stock of 3000 bananas, what is the maximum number of bananas that the camel can transport across the desert and into the eager hands of waiting customers who live in the exotic city?

1.5 Word Morphing with Lewis Carroll

Lewis Carroll—mathematician, teacher, and author of Alice in Wonderland—invented a marvelous word game in the 1870s that he called "Doublets". Nowadays, I'll call it word morphing. Here is how it goes: Take two words having the same number of letters, say **cat** and **dog**. Can you transform (morph) the **cat** into a **dog** by changing only one letter at a time where each intermediate form is a bona-fide word in the English language? **Cat** and **dog** are easy. Consider the sequence—**cat**, **cot**, **dot**, and **dog**—which solves the problem quite nicely. Again, every word in the sequence (Carroll called this a chain) must be an English word, and the player can only change one letter at a time. Also, the original rules prohibit switching letters within a word. Here is another example; to turn **warm** into **cold**, construct the sequence: **warm**, **ward**, **card**, **cord**, and **cold**. One can have fun anywhere and almost anytime with Lewis Carroll's wonderful little word game!

Challenge: Back in Carroll's day, nobody could take the **horse** to the **field**. I am now told that English words are available that can make this chain happen—your move!

1.6 The Three Bears

Which of the following sentences, if any, bears errors?

1) No bear bare should bare a burden.
2) No bear bare should bear a burden.
3) No bare bear should bear a burden.

1.7 Here Lies Old Diophantus

The Greek Mathematician Diophantus of Alexander (born about 200 AD) is considered by many historians to be the father of algebra. He wrote a book called <u>Arithmetica</u>, the earliest written record containing variables, algebraic equations, and solutions. There is an epithet for Diophantus (published about 500 AD) describing his life in terms of a riddle: "This tomb holds Diophantus. Ah, how great a marvel! The tomb tells scientifically the measure of his life. Zeus granted him to be a boy for one-sixth of his life, and adding a twelfth part to this, Zeus clothed his cheeks with down. He lit him the light of wedlock after a seventh part, and five years after his marriage Zeus gave him a son. Alas, late-born wretched child! After obtaining the measure of half his father's life, chill Fate took him. After, consoling his grief by the study of numbers for four years, Diophantus ended his life." *From this riddle, can you determine how old Diophantus was when he died?*

1.8 Young Gauss Stuns His Teacher

Carl Gauss (1777-1855) is considered by many to be one of the greatest mathematicians of all time. Legend has it that he entered school at the age of 5 and stunned his teacher who gave him a tedious problem to solve, thinking it would take the lad an hour or more. Here is the problem: add the counting numbers 1 through 100. The answer is 5050, and Gauss had determined it within one minute! *How did young Gauss solve the problem so quickly?*

1.9 One Dollar Please

The following logic puzzle is very old. It always seems to challenge each new generation of thinkers as the story line gets updated to fit changing times. Three men stayed for one night in a motel, all three sharing the same room. They checked out the next morning, the bill for the night coming to $25.00. Each man gave the motel clerk a $10.00 bill and told him to keep $2.00 of the change as a tip. The clerk gave $1.00 in change back to each of the three men. A quick reckoning has the night costing $27.00 plus a $2.00 tip. *Where did the other dollar go?*

1.10 Four Fours Puzzle

Challenge: Create all the counting numbers 0 through 100 using mathematical equalities having exactly four 4s and no other numerals on the left hand side. Two examples are

$$4x4x4 - 4 = 60$$
and
$$4 \div 4 + 4! + \sqrt{4} = 27.$$

1.11 My Problem with Ice Cream

My problem with ice cream is that I love it, and I always have! The problem below is for all ice-cream lovers. And, if you are a true ice-cream lover, I can imagine you saying, "Not a problem!" Now, the local ice-cream parlor sells monster once-in-a-lifetime sundaes for those very special occasions. A customer is allowed to pick from three flavors: chewy double chocolate crunch ($1.00 per scoop), multi-berry ambrosia ($1.60 per scoop), and Aegean vanilla ($.80 per scoop). A monster sundae costs $20.00, $16.00 for 15 scoops of ice cream and an additional $4.00 for an assortment of delectable toppings. *In how many different ways can I order my monthly—oops—treat? What are they? Note: the parlor will not serve partial scoops.*

1.12 Word Squares

Word squares, which were very popular throughout the 1800s, are the language equivalent of magic squares and the forerunners to the modern crossword puzzle. Below are five word squares of various sizes.

		2x2 ON NO	
3x3	**4x4**	**5x5**	**6x6**
BAG	LANE	STUNG	CIRCLE
APE	AREA	TENOR	ICARUS
GET	NEAR	UNTIE	RAREST
	EARS	NOISE	CREATE
		GREET	LUSTRE
			ESTEEM

As shown, each square is composed of words of equal length that read in exactly the same way both horizontally and vertically. Diagonals do not have to be words. The 6x6 above is famous because when it first appeared in 1859, it claimed—tongue in cheek—to have solved the problem of "squaring the circle" (see note below). 7x7, 8x8, and 9x9 word squares are in existence today—but no 10x10!

Challenge: Try to construct a word square consisting of words unique to your family, town, favorite sports team, etc. in such a way that all the words support the same general idea. *Super Challenge*: Construct a 10x10 word square and become famous! Gain entry into <u>Ripley's Believe it or Not!</u>

1.13 The 100 Puzzle

The 100 Puzzle is a very old favorite which can be used in the middle grades as an arithmetic enrichment exercise. Here is how it goes. First, write the digits one through nine in natural order. Now, without moving any of the nine digits, insert arithmetic signs and/or parenthesis so that the digits total to 100. Dudeney, one of the greatest puzzles creators of all times, claimed that

$$1+2+3+4+5+6+7+(8x9)=100$$

was the most common solution. He came up with many solutions during his lifetime including this favorite:

$$123-45-67+89=100.$$

Dudeney liked this particular solution because it minimized the number of arithmetic signs.

Yet another solution is $12+3-4+5+67+8+9=100$.

Things to try:

1) Conduct a contest to see who can come up with the most solutions.
2) Conduct a contest to see who can come up with a solution having a minimum number of signs.
3) Reverse the digits one through nine (writing them in decreasing order) and play The Reverse 100 Puzzle.

   One solution is $98+7-6+5-4+3-2-1=100$.

4) Write the nine digits in random order and play 1) and 2) above.

1.14 Coloring the Grid

The object is to color the 4 by 4 grid shown below where 4 of the little squares are to be blue, 3 are to be green, 3 are to be white, 3 are to be yellow, and 3 are to be red. *Challenge*: Color the grid so none of the five colors appears more than once in any horizontal, vertical, or main-diagonal line.

1.15 The 3X3 Anti-Magic Square

The 3X3 magic square has the property that the three numbers in each of the three rows, three columns, and two diagonals (eight sums altogether) add up to 15.

Challenge: Using the digits one through nine, construct an opposing 3X3 anti-magic square where no two sums are alike.

2	7	6	?	?	?
9	5	1	?	?	?
4	3	8	?	?	?

1.16 The Famous Girder Problem

The problem below started to appear in calculus texts circa 1900. My father first experienced it in 1930 as an engineering student, and I first encountered it in the winter of 1966. It still appears in modern calculus textbooks disguised—and somewhat watered down—as a geometric optimization problem. The girder problem is famous because of the way it thoroughly integrates the principles of plane geometry, algebra, and differential calculus. My experience as a teacher has been that "many try, but few succeed. " Will you? Have fun!

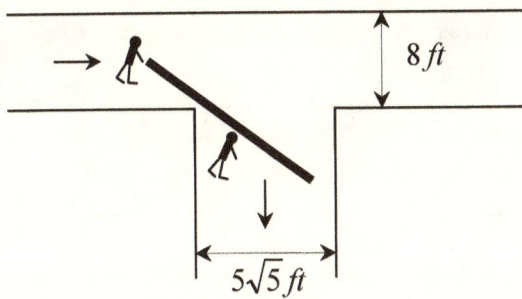

The problem and the challenge: Two people at a construction site are rolling steel beams down a corridor 8 feet wide into a second corridor $5\sqrt{5}$ feet wide and perpendicular to the first corridor. What is the length of the longest girder that can be rolled from the first corridor into the second corridor and continued on its journey in the construction site? Assume the beam is of negligible thickness.

1.17 No Calculators Allowed!

Use the techniques of differential calculus to show that $e^{\pi} > \pi^{e}$.

91

1.18 A Mathematician's Desert

A frequent problem in first term calculus is to find the area of the largest rectangle that can be inscribed inside the first-quadrant portion of the unit circle. See the figure on the left below. For those of you who haven't worked with calculus for a while, I suggest that this well-known problem (which is solved using single-variable differential calculus) be your warm-up.

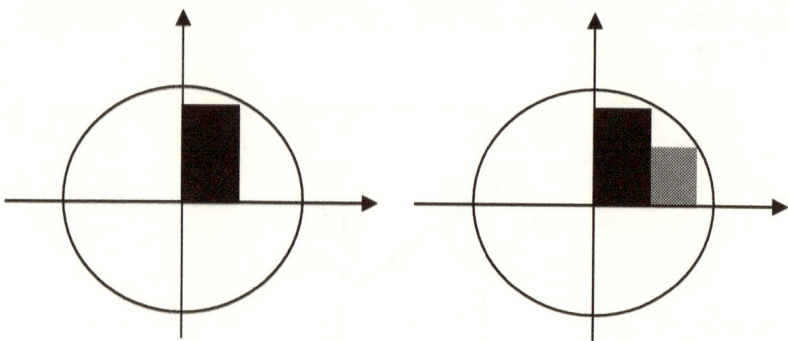

Challenge: It doesn't take much of an expansion to turn the above problem into a connoisseur's absolute delight consisting of two independent variables, partial derivatives, and subtle observations—not to mention a king-sized scoop of algebra. Here it comes! The figure on the right is joined to the following question: Find the dimensions for each of the two rectangles inscribed in the unit circle as shown that maximizes the total combined area of both rectangles.

Note: An Air Force Captain first introduced me to this problem in 1981 after experiencing it on a Ph.D. qualifying examination the week before. Thanks Joe for a superb treat!

1.19 Triple Play

Calculus is always more fun when two or three variables are in the game. The problem below is similar to the one presented in "A Mathematician's Desert", but we have added one more variable to the lineup!

Challenge: Consider the figure below where the equation of the line segment is given by $y = 1 - x$ where $0 \leq x \leq 1$.

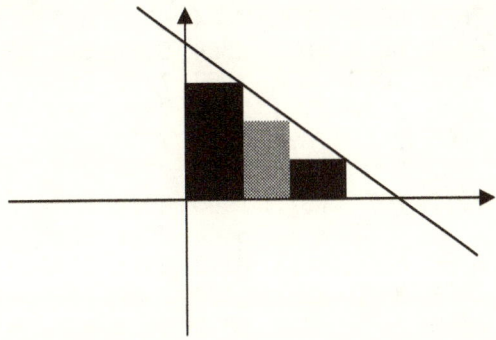

Find the dimensions for each of the three rectangles inscribed in the triangular region as shown that maximizes the total combined area of the threesome.

1.20 Calling all Data Lovers

There is a small, well-kept cemetery close to where I live—the final resting-place for 180 (last count) Catholic priests and brothers. Below is the data summary from all 180 headstones. Each four-digit entry is the year of death (with the 19 omitted) and age at death. For example, the first entry 6245 codes a death in 1962 at age 45.

6245, 6286, 6338, 6346, 6383, 6393, 6462, 6464, 6475, 6488,
6557, 6671, 6679, 6682, 6763, 6784, 6832, 6839, 6846, 6854,
6866, 6876, 6877, 6877, 6883, 6884, 6952, 6957, 6984, 7033,
7059, 7065, 7072, 7079, 7086, 7087, 7143, 7167, 7168, 7176,
7182, 7189, 7236, 7252, 7261, 7275, 7287, 7288, 7356, 7369,
7462, 7467, 7468, 7471, 7474, 7478, 7550, 7666, 7667, 7667,
7676, 7678, 7682, 7690, 7741, 7764, 7774, 7775, 7784, 7967,
7968, 7969, 7972, 7974, 7977, 7990, 8082, 8084, 8164, 8167,
8170, 8172, 8182, 8182, 8183, 8184, 8191, 8246, 8259, 8266,
8275, 8276, 8286, 8290, 8294, 8373, 8376, 8378, 8385, 8468,
8474, 8477, 8479, 8480, 8567, 8569, 8569, 8569, 8570, 8579,
8580, 8584, 8666, 8672, 8673, 8678, 8681, 8769, 8769, 8774,
8781, 8790, 8864, 8870, 8878, 8888, 8889, 8954, 8973, 8973,
8979, 8990, 8993, 9067, 9082, 9083, 9088, 9149, 9155, 9171,
9176, 9181, 9183, 9260, 9276, 9294, 9357, 9368, 9380, 9380,
9385, 9390, 9392, 9467, 9471, 9483, 9483, 9484, 9486, 9486,
9568, 9580, 9583, 9583, 9584, 9658, 9662, 9677, 9677, 9678,
9679, 9680, 9682, 9684, 9686, 9689, 9693, 9781, 9788, 9797:
R.I.P.

Challenge: can you argue a case for increasing male longevity in the United States from this particular sample? Why or why not? Let statistics (or sadistics as some of my students like to say) be your guide.

94

2) Curios

2.1 Twin Towers Numerology

The following number curios were sent to me shortly after the World Trade Center bombing. We humans are always seeking meaning and significance in those tragic or happy events that affect our lives. The establishing of numerical patterns is one way (and a very ancient one) that people use to explore meaning.

1. The date of the attack: 9/11 = 9+1+1 = 11
2. September 11, 254th day of the year: 2+5+4 = 11
3. After September 11, 111 days are left in the year
4. 119 is the area code for Iran/Iraq: 1+1+9 = 11
5. The Twin Towers looked like the number 11
6. The first plane to hit the towers was Flight 11
7. The 11th state added to the Union was New York
8. New York City has 11 letters
9. Afghanistan has 11 letters
10. "The Pentagon" has 11 letters
11. Ramzi Yousef has 11 letters (convicted in the World Trade Center bombing of 1993)
12. Flight 11 had 92 people on board: 9+2 = 11
13. Flight 77 had 65 on board: 6+5 = 11

A question to ponder: Is there a significant event in your life where you have used numerical patterns (perhaps dates) to help establish meaning? Martin Gardner (of Scientific American fame) has given the name jiggery-pokery to such quests for numerological patterns. Jiggery-pokery or not, we will continue as rational beings to seek and establish patterns of all sorts.

II

2.2 A Potpourri of Powers

After seeing the Pythagorean relationship between three squares, one might ask what other neat relationships exist amongst numbers, multiples, digits, and powers. Below is a connoisseur's sampling. Enjoy, and if you don't believe one of the statements below, then check it out!

1. $6^3 = 3^3 + 4^3 + 5^3$

2. $49 = 47 + 2$ and $94 = 47x2$

3. $371 = 3^3 + 7^3 + 1^3$ and $407 = 4^3 + 0^3 + 7^3$

4. $135 = 1^1 + 3^2 + 5^3$ and $175 = 1^1 + 7^2 + 5^3$

5. $169 = 13^2$ and $961 = 31^2$

6. $244 = 1^3 + 3^3 + 6^3$ and $136 = 2^3 + 4^3 + 4^3$

7. $499 = 497 + 2$ and $994 = 497x2$

8. $504 = 12x42 = 21x24$

9. $1634 = 1^4 + 6^4 + 3^4 + 4^4$ and $3435 = 3^3 + 4^4 + 3^3 + 5^5$

10. $2025 = 45^2$ and $20 + 25 = 45$

11. $4913 = 17^3$ and $4 + 9 + 1 + 3 = 17$

12. 9240 has 64 divisors

13. $54,748 = 5^5 + 4^5 + 7^5 + 4^5 + 8^5$

14. $321489 = 567^2$ Other than the exponent, this equality uses each of the nine digits just once.

15. First Eight **Rare** *Perfect Numbers* where the sum of all proper divisors for the number equals the number itself:

6	8128	
28	33550336	137438691328
496	8589869056	2305843008139952128

2.3 Narcissistic Numbers

According to Greek mythology, Narcissus fell in love with his own image while looking into a pool of water. He subsequently turned into a flower that "bears" his name. Narcissistic numbers are numbers whose own digits can be used to recreate themselves via established rules of arithmetic. A lovely sampling is below—all waiting to be verified by the willing student! Also included are three examples of "narcissistic pairs".

1. $3435 = 3^3 + 4^4 + 3^3 + 5^5$
2. $127 = -1 + 2^7$
3. $598 = 5^1 + 9^2 + 8^3$
4. $3125 = (3^1 + 2)^5$
5. $1676 = 1^1 + 6^2 + 7^3 + 6^4 = 1^5 + 6^4 + 7^3 + 6^2$
6. $759375 = (7 - 5 + 9 - 3 + 7)^5$
7. $2592 = 2^5 \cdot 9^2$
8. $1233 = 12^2 + 33^2$
9. $990100 = 990^2 + 100^2$
10. $94122353 = 9412^2 + 2353^2$
11. $2646798 = 2^1 + 6^2 + 4^3 + 6^4 + 7^5 + 9^6 + 8^7$
12. $2427 = 2^1 + 4^2 + 2^3 + 7^4$
13. $24739 = 2^4 \cdot 7! \cdot 3^9$
14. $3869 = 62^2 + 05^2$ & $6205 = 38^2 + 69^2$ *pair*
15. $5965 = 77^2 + 06^2$ & $7706 = 59^2 + 65^2$ *pair*
16. $244 = 1^3 + 3^3 + 6^3$ & $136 = 2^3 + 4^3 + 4^3$ *pair*
17. $343 = (3 + 4)^3$
18. $221859 = 22^3 + 18^3 + 59^3$
19. $416768 = 768^2 - 416^2$
20. $3468 = 68^2 - 34^2$

2.4 Numerology of 666

The number 666 has been in Western thought for about twenty centuries. In Roman times, 666 would have been easily written in Roman times as DCLXVI, a simple descending sequence of the first six Roman numerals. Today, writing 654321 would serve the same purpose. The number 666 has many fascinating numerical properties, eight of which are listed below.

1. $666 = 6 + 6 + 6 + 6^3 + 6^3 + 6^3$

2. $666 = 1^6 - 2^6 + 3^6$

3. $666 = 2^2 + 3^2 + 5^2 + 7^2 + 11^2 + 13^2 + 17^2$: The sum of the squares of the first seven prime numbers

4. $666 = 313 + 353$: The sum of two consecutive prime numbers that read the same forward and backward).

5. $666 = 2x3x3x37$ and $6 + 6 + 6 = 2 + 3 + 3 + 3 + 7$. 666 is called a Smith number since the sum of its digits is equal to the sum of the digits of its prime factors.

6. $666^2 = 443556$ and $666^3 = 295408296$. Furthermore,
$$\left(4^2 + 4^2 + 3^2 + 5^2 + 5^2 + 6^2\right) +$$
$$(2 + 9 + 5 + 4 + 0 + 8 + 2 + 9 + 6) = 666$$

7. 666 is made from the ascending sequence 123456789 by insertion of one or more plus signs in two different ways:
$$1 + 2 + 3 + 4 + 567 + 89 = 666$$
$$123 + 456 + 78 + 9 = 666$$

8. 666 is made from the descending sequence 987654321 by $666 = 9 + 87 + 6 + 543 + 21$.

2.5 False Demonstration: Two Equals One

Step 1: Set $x = y$

Step 2: Multiply both sides by x: $x^2 = yx$

Step 3: Subtract y^2 from both sides: $x^2 - y^2 = xy - y^2$

Step 4: Factor both sides: $(x - y)(x + y) = y(x - y)$

Step 5: Divide both sides by $x - y$: $x + y = y$

Step 6: Substitute $x = y$ from Step 1: $2y = y$

Step 7: Dividing both sides by y results in $2 = 1$ $\therefore$

2.6 Selected Magic Squares

1. 3X3 Magic Square: Magic Sum is 15.

2	7	6
9	5	1
4	3	8

2. 4X4 Perfect Magic Square: Magic Sum is 34.

1	15	6	12
8	10	3	13
11	5	16	2
14	4	9	7

3. 5X5 Perfect Magic Square: Magic Sum is 65.

1	15	8	24	17
23	7	16	5	14
20	4	13	22	6
12	21	10	19	3
9	18	2	11	25

Note: For a Magic Square of size NXN, the Magic Sum is given by the formula

$$\frac{N(N^2 + 1)}{2}.$$

4. Nested 5X5 Magic Square: Outer Magic Sum is 65.

1	18	21	22	3
2	10	17	12	24
18	15	13	11	8
21	14	9	16	5
23	7	6	4	25

5. 6X6 Magic Square: Magic Sum is 111.

1	32	3	34	35	6
12	29	9	10	26	25
13	14	22	21	23	18
24	20	16	15	17	19
30	11	28	27	8	7
31	5	33	4	2	36

6. 7X7 Magic Square: Magic Sum is 175.

22	21	13	5	46	38	30
31	23	15	14	6	47	39
40	32	24	16	8	7	48
49	31	33	25	17	9	1
2	43	42	34	26	18	10
11	3	44	36	35	27	19
20	12	4	45	37	29	28

7. Ben Franklin's 8X8 *Almost* Magic Square:

52	61	04	13	20	29	36	45
14	03	62	51	46	35	30	19
53	60	05	12	21	28	37	44
11	06	59	54	43	38	27	22
55	58	07	10	23	26	39	42
09	08	57	56	41	40	25	24
50	63	02	15	18	31	34	47
16	01	64	49	48	33	32	17

8. Quadruple-Nested 9X9 Magic Square:
   Outer Magic Sum is 369.

16	81	79	78	77	13	12	11	2
76	28	65	62	61	26	27	18	6
75	23	36	53	51	35	30	59	7
74	24	50	40	45	38	32	58	8
9	25	33	39	41	43	49	57	73
10	60	34	44	37	42	48	22	72
14	63	52	29	31	47	46	19	68
15	64	17	20	21	56	55	54	67
80	1	3	4	5	69	70	71	66

2.7 Curry's Missing Square Paradox

Two identical sets consisting of four pieces each are used to
construct both figures

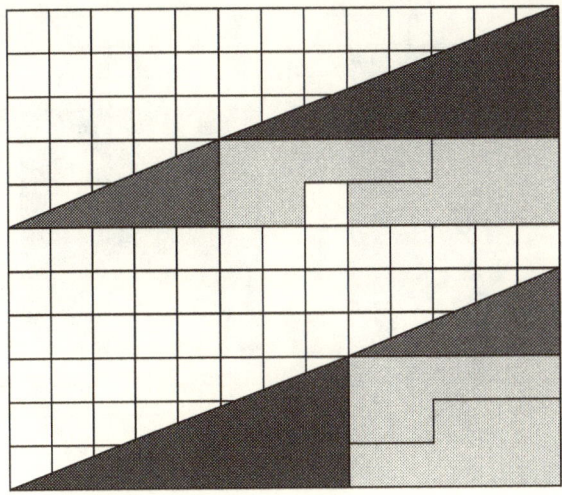

2.8 Tangram Missing Area Paradox

Identical Tangram sets consisting of the seven traditional pieces
are used to construct both figures.

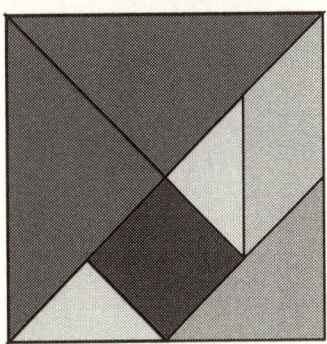 

2.9 Square/Rectangle Gaining Area Paradox

Two identical sets consisting of four pieces each are used to
construct both figures

2.10 The Twelve Pentominoes

The twelve pieces are all possible fusions of five squares.

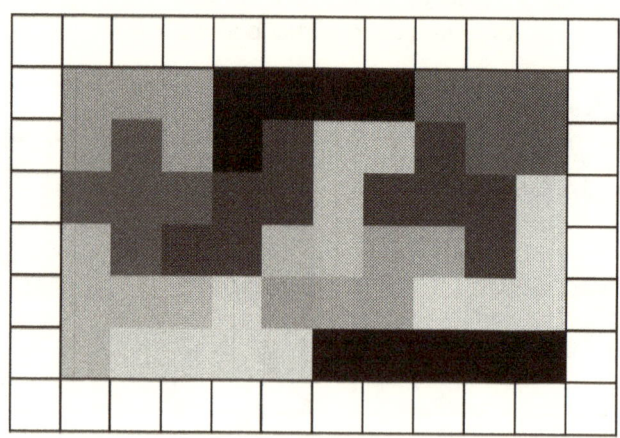

2.11 1885 Arithmetic Exam

If you wanted to *enter* Jersey City High School back in 1885, you first had to pass an entrance exam covering five basic academic disciplines: arithmetic, geography, United States history, English grammar, and algebra. The ten questions below comprise the 1885 arithmetic exam.

1. If a 60-days note of $840.00 is discounted at 4.5% by a bank, what are the proceeds?
2. The interest on $50.00 from 1 March to 1 July is $2.50. What is the annual simple interest rate?
3. The mason work on a building can be finished by 16 men in 24 hours, working 10 hours a day. How long will it take 22 men working 8 hours a day?
4. By selling goods at 12.5% profit, a man clears $800.00. How much did they cost? For how much were they sold?
5. What is the cost of 83 pounds of sugar at $98.50 a ton?
6. A merchant sold some goods at a 5% discount for $18,775.00 and still made a 10% profit. What did the merchant pay for the goods?
7. Find the sum of $\sqrt{16.7281}$ and $\sqrt{.721\frac{1}{4}}$
8. Find $(.37 - .095) \div (.00025)$. Express the result in words.
9. A requires 10 days and B 15 days to paint a house. How long will it take A and B together to paint the house?
10. A merchant offered some goods for $1170.90 cash, or $1206 payable in 30 days. Find the simple interest rate.

2.12 1885 Algebra Exam

The ten questions below comprise the algebra portion from the same 1885 Jersey City High School entrance exam.

1. Define algebra, algebraic expression, and polynomial.
2. Simplify the following expression:
$$1-(1-a)+(1-a+a^2)-(1-a+a^2-a^3).$$
3. Find the product of the two expressions
$$3+4x+5x^2-6x^3 \text{ and } 4-5x-6x^2.$$
4. Write a homogeneous quadrinomial of the third degree.
5. Express the cube root of $10ax$ in two ways.
6. Find the prime factors of a) x^4-b^4 and b) x^3-1.
7. Find both the sum and difference of the two expressions
$$3x-4ay+7cd-4xy+16 \ \&$$
$$10ay-3x-8xy+7cd-13.$$
8. Divide the expression $6a^4+4xa^3-9(ax)^2-3ax^3$ by the expression $2a^2+2ax-x^2$ and check.

9. Find the Greatest Common Divisor (G.C.D.) for the two expressions $6a^2+11ax+3x^2$ and $6a^2+7ax-3x^2$.

10. Divide $\dfrac{x^2-2xy+y^2}{ab}$ by $\dfrac{x-y}{bc}$ and give the answer in its lowest terms.

2.13 1947 Algebra Exam

Below is the algebra portion of a Canadian high school exit exam from the year 1947. A score of 80% was required to pass. How do you score in this century?

1. Prove: $\log_a N^p = p \log_a N$.

2. Plot the graphs of $y = 3x^2 - x^3$ and $y = 3x + 7$ on the same set of axis for the interval $-1 \le x \le 4$. Prove that $y = x^3 - 3x^2 + 3x + 7$ has one real root and find it.

3. If $\dfrac{x}{y}$ varies as $(x + y)$ and $\dfrac{y}{x}$ varies as $x^2 - xy + y^2$, show that $x^3 + y^3$ is a constant.

4. Prove: $a + (a + d) + (a + 2d) + \ldots = \dfrac{n}{2}\left(2a + [9n - 1]d\right)$.

5. If $P_n^5 = 90 P_{n-2}^3$, find the value of n.

6. How many even numbers of four digits can be formed with the numerals 2, 3, 4, 5, 6, if no numeral is used more than once in each number?

7. If m and n are the roots of the quadratic equation $ax^2 + bx + c = 0$, prove that $m + n = -\dfrac{b}{a}, mn = \dfrac{c}{a}$.

8. One root of the equation $x^2 - (3a + 2)x + 12 = 3$ is three times the other. Find the value of a.

9. Expand $\dfrac{1}{(1 - 3x)^2}$ to 4 terms in ascending powers of x.

10. Show that when higher powers of x can be neglected, $\dfrac{\sqrt{1 + x} + \sqrt[3]{(1 - x)^2}}{1 + x + \sqrt{1 + x}}$ is approximately $1 - \dfrac{5}{6}x$.

2.14 2004 Monster Algebra Exam

1. Solve the following equations:

a) $\dfrac{1}{w} = \dfrac{1}{x} + \dfrac{1}{y} + \dfrac{1}{z}$ for w b) $2\sqrt{x-3} + \sqrt{3x-5} = 8$

c) $\sqrt{\dfrac{x-3}{x-8}} - \dfrac{x}{\sqrt{x+4}} = -\dfrac{3}{2}$ d) $\sqrt[4]{5x^2 - 6} = x$

e) $\dfrac{x^2}{x^2 - 5x + 6} = \dfrac{2}{x-2} + \dfrac{6}{(x-2)(x-3)}$

2. Evaluate the following two expressions.

a) $\dfrac{(7.25)^{1359} \times \sqrt{(7.14)^{13.5}}}{(3.39)^{1481}}$ b) $\dfrac{(9.2)^{545} \times (5.33459)^{24.79}}{(4.15)^{934} \times \sqrt[7]{519.395}}$

3. A rectangular solid has the length of each side increased by the same amount in order to double the volume. Find the revised dimensions if the original dimensions are 3 by 4 by 5 cm.

4. A plane left an airfield to fly to a destination 1860 miles away. After flying at an unknown airspeed for 600 miles, the wind changed increasing the airspeed of the plane by 40 mph. This reduced the time of the trip by 45 minutes. What was the original airspeed of the plane?

5. A dealer bought a shipment of shoes for $480.00. He sold all but 5 pairs at a profit of $6.00 per pair, thereby making a total profit of $290.00 on the shipment. How many pairs of shoes were in the original shipment?

6. Two train stations A and B are 300 miles apart and in the same time zone. At 5AM a passenger train leaves A for B and a freight train leaves B for A. The two trains meet at a point 100 miles from B. Had the speed of the passenger train been 10 mph faster, it would have reached B 9 hours before the fright train reached A. How fast was each train traveling?

2.15 Ten Commandments of Algebra

Algebra can be thought of as a language, universal in scope! Many people are frustrated when learning this language because they fail to follow a few basic study rules. Here are ten such rules written in yesterday's English.

1. Thou shall read thy problem.
2. Whatsoever thou shall do to one side of the equation, do thou also to the other side.
3. Thou shall draw a picture when doing a word problem in order to actively engage both sides of thy brain.
4. Thou shall ignore the teachings of false prophets to do complicated work in thy head.
5. Thou must use thy 'Common Sense', or else thou wilt have flagpoles 9000 feet in height, yea... even fathers younger than sons.
6. When thou art clueless, thou shall look it up; and if thy search is fruitless, thou shall ask the teacher.
7. Thou shall master each step before putting down in haste thy heavy foot on the next.
8. Thy correct answer does not always prove that thou has understood or correctly worked the problem.
9. The shall first see that thou has copied thy problem correctly before bearing false witness that the book is a father of lies.
10. Thou shall look back even to thy youth and remember thy arithmetic.

3) Answers to Selected Puzzles

1.1

1.2

1)

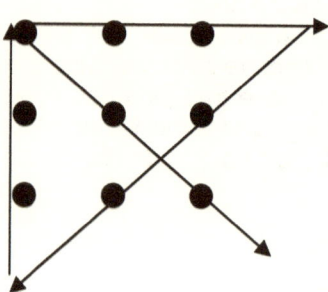

2) 30 squares total

1.3

Wolf, Goat, Cabbage: F, W, G, C: F, G cross; F comes back; F, W cross; F, G come back; F, C cross; F comes back; F, G cross for the last time.

U2: E, B cross (2 minutes); E comes back (2 minute); A, L cross (10 minutes), B comes back (1 minute), E, B cross for the second time (2 minutes). The times total 17 minutes.

1.4

533 1/3 bananas

1.7

84 years old

1.9

Stage	3 Men	Hotel	Bell	Sum
1) Before entering	30	0	0	30
2) Front Desk	0	30	0	30
3) Send Back	0	25	5	30
4) Distribution	3	25	2	30

1.14

G	W	B	Y
B	Y	R	G
R	G	W	B
W	B	Y	R

1.15

Unlike the magic square, the solution below is only one of many.

2	4	7
5	1	8
9	3	6

1.16

Exactly 27 feet

1.17

Hint, analyze $f(x) = e^x - x^e$ on the interval $0 \le x \le \infty$.

1.18

See diagram below. Note the definitions of X and Y!

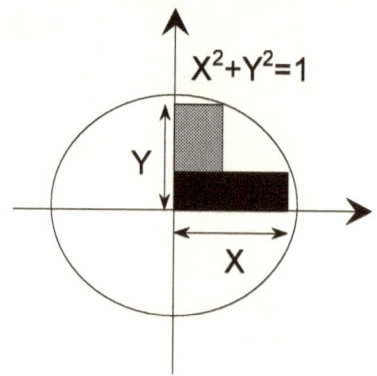

Let $A(x, y) = x\sqrt{1-x^2} + (y - \sqrt{1-x^2})\sqrt{1-y^2}$.

Set $\dfrac{\partial A}{\partial X} = \dfrac{\partial A}{\partial y} = 0 \Rightarrow X = Y = .85$ (rounded to two decimals).

1.19

Set up $A(x, y, z) = x(1-x) + (y-x)(1-y) + (z-y)(1-z)$ and optimize for the region $0 \leq x \leq y \leq z \leq 1$.

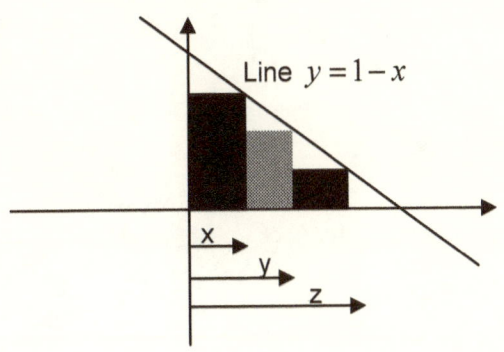

Line $y = 1 - x$

1.20

Just one example of what is possible

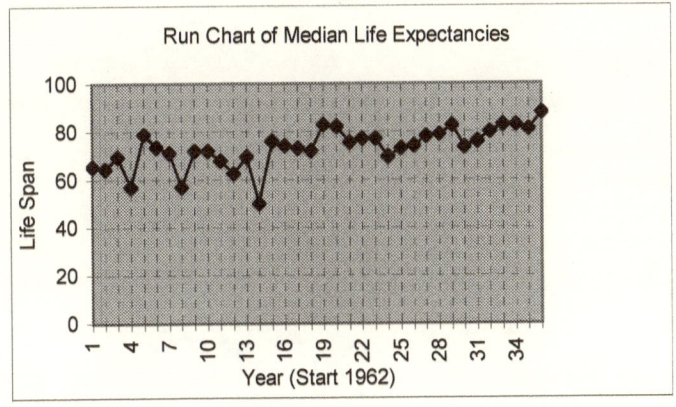

113

My Most-Used Formulas

Formula   Page Ref

1.

2.

3.

4.

5.

6.

7.

8.

9.

10.

11.

12.

www.ingramcontent.com/pod-product-compliance
Lightning Source LLC
Chambersburg PA
CBHW021544290526
45785CB00004BA/1509